At Issue

Has No Child Left
Behind Been Good
for Education?

Other Books in the At Issue Series:

At Issue

Has No Child Left Behind Been Good for Education?

Christina Fisanick, Book Editor

GREENHAVEN PRESS
A part of Gale, Cengage Learning

Detroit • New York • San Francisco • New Haven, Conn • Waterville, Maine • London

Christine Nasso, *Publisher*
Elizabeth Des Chenes, *Managing Editor*

For more information, contact:
Greenhaven Press
27500 Drake Rd.
Farmington Hills, MI 48331-3535
Or you can visit our Internet site at gale.cengage.com

For product information and technology assistance, contact us at

Gale Customer Support, 1-800-877-4253
For permission to use material from this text or product, submit all requests online at www.cengage.com/permissions

Further permissions questions can be emailed to permissionrequest@cengage.com

Articles in Greenhaven Press anthologies are often edited for length to meet page requirements. In addition, original titles of these works are changed to clearly present the main thesis and to explicitly indicate the author's opinion. Every effort is made to ensure that Greenhaven Press accurately reflects the original intent of the authors. Every effort has been made to trace the owners of copyrighted material.

Cover photograph reproduced by permission of © Todd Davidson/Illustration Works/Corbis.

LIBRARY OF CONGRESS CATALOGING-IN-PUBLICATION DATA

Has No Child Left Behind Been Good for Education? / Christina Fisanick, book editor.
   p. cm. -- (At issue)
  Includes bibliographical references and index.
  ISBN-13: 978-0-7377-3920-6 (hardcover)
  ISBN-13: 978-0-7377-3921-3 (pbk.)
  1. United States. No Child Left Behind Act of 2001. 2. Educational accountability --Law and legislation--United States. 3. Education--Standards--United States. 4. Education--United States--Evaluation. 5. Educational equalization--United States. I. Fisanick, Christina.
  LB2806.22.H37 2008
  379.1'580973--dc22
                                       2007050859

Printed in the United States of America
1 2 3 4 5 6 7 12 11 10 09 08

Contents

Introduction

Signed into law on January 8, 2002, after being passed through the House of Representatives in late 2001, the No Child Left Behind Act (NCLB) has become one of the nation's most controversial education reforms. NCLB is a revision of the Elementary and Secondary Education Act (ESEA) of 1965, which provided federal aid to schools with large populations of low-income students. Although the federal government developed assessment tools for following student progress under ESEA, it did not tie funding to achievement in the way that NCLB does. Many arguments have been and are continuing to be made for and against the Act, and teacher quality has become a main focus of these debates.

Excellent teachers are an obvious necessity for strong educational programs. According to the Education Trust, a national education advocacy group, "Effective teachers can help students make enormous gains, while ineffective teachers can do lasting damage." Determining what it means to be a good teacher is a complex issue, however. NCLB guidelines define "highly qualified teachers" as education professionals who hold a bachelor's degree from an accredited institution, obtain full state licensure or certification, and demonstrate proficiency in each subject they teach. All teachers nationwide were to have met these criteria by the 2005–2006 school year, but this goal was not attained. In an effort to ensure that more teachers become highly qualified, President George W. Bush added $2.9 billion to his 2007 budget for state programs aimed at increasing teaching excellence.

Although these criteria might seem straightforward and worthwhile, a number of critics have argued that overemphasis on the details of these requirements has actually led to less effective teaching. Roy E. Barnes and Joseph A. Aguerrebere Jr., commentators for *Education Week*, note that too much focus on calculating credit hours spent taking certain courses and background checks "has become an exercise in meeting the lowest common denominator of quality." Rather than measuring effective instruction, detractors argue that NCLB-imposed guidelines provide mere checklists for keeping otherwise good teachers out of the classroom. One such teacher is Jefferds Huyck. Huyck was dismissed from his job teaching Latin at a California high school because he lacked certification. According to an article by Samuel Freedman in the *New York Times*, Huyck holds a PhD in Classics from Harvard, had been teaching high school for more than twenty years, and his students had demonstrated measurable academic success. He decided against going through the certification process because of the time and expense required to complete the program.

Nonetheless, many proponents of NCLB argue that without the highly-qualified-teacher requirements, students will continue to suffer, especially low-income and minority students. Providing highly qualified teachers is important to closing this gap, but even after years of NCLB implementation, it has been noted that low-income and minority students are still being underserved. In a report released in August 2007 by the U.S. Department of Education and the American Institutes for Research, principal research analyst Kerstin Le Floch noted that "although a high percentage of teachers are considered highly qualified, the results tend to mask some problem areas." The study revealed that teachers in schools that serve predominately disadvantaged students were less likely to be classified as highly qualified under NCLB. Even among those teachers deemed highly qualified, teachers in impoverished areas often had very little teaching experience and many did not have degrees in the subject areas in which they taught. Therefore, developing and measuring standards of teaching excellence is even more important in helping historically underprivileged students succeed.

Some critics argue that teacher quality should be measured, but they also insist that there are better ways of doing so. Researchers at the Center for Teacher Quality, a national organization devoted to assessing and improving teaching practices, argue that "teachers who meet their states' definitions of 'highly qualified' under the NCLB Act do not necessarily teach in ways that will allow their students to meet rigorous academic standards." The Commission on No Child Left Behind, which conducted a large scale study of the effectiveness of the Act, concluded that simply measuring qualifications is not the same as measuring qualities. According to the commission's report, "It is time to ensure that all teachers demonstrate their effectiveness in the classroom rather than just their qualifications for entering it." Still, critics argue that the even these improvements are limited because they rely too heavily on student test scores to determine teacher success and not the less measurable qualities of good teaching, such as character building and compassion.

It remains to be seen whether NCLB will be reauthorized as is, completely overhauled, or allowed to expire. (As of January 2008, reauthorization procedures had stalled in Congress). While NCLB is being discussed disagreements about its effectiveness are sure to continue. Given that billions of dollars in federal funding and the future of America's children are at stake, it is a cause worthy of serious debate. In *At Issue: Has No Child Left Behind Been Good for Education?* the authors present a variety of perspectives on the Act's effectiveness, including funding, testing, and serving students with special needs.

1

No Child Left Behind Is Adequately and Appropriately Funded

U.S. House of Representatives Committee on Education and Labor

The House Committee on Education and Labor oversees education and workforce programs that impact hundreds of millions of Americans, including teachers, students, small-business operators, and retirees.

Throughout the history of the American educational system, schools and school districts have not been held accountable for student or teacher performance. The No Child Left Behind Act (NCLB) changes that practice by linking funding to achievement. Not only have federal funds for education increased since NCLB, but in some cases the law may be overfunded. Although the NCLB funding structure encourages school participation, states may opt out of the program and decline the money. Therefore, NCLB is not an unfunded mandate but an optional tool designed to help schools better serve their students.

If money were the solution to the problems in America's schools, those problems would have been solved long ago. But money isn't the solution. That's why President [George W.] Bush and Congress enacted the No Child Left Behind Act (NCLB). In enacting NCLB, President Bush and Republicans promised education funding would increase, and would be linked for the first time to accountability for results. This is exactly what has occurred.

U.S. House of Representatives Committee on Education and Labor, "No Child Left Behind Is Funded," in http://republicans.edlabor.house.gov, January 4, 2007.

No more spending without accountability. Prior to NCLB, states accepted billions of dollars a year in federal education aid, but were not held accountable for using that money to get academic results for all children. Disadvantaged students were written off as unteachable and shuffled through the system without receiving a quality education—and federal law endorsed this practice. Millions of parents were denied the ability to know whether or not their children were learning, and denied the ability to do anything about it if they suspected their children's schools weren't getting the job done.

A one-third increase in federal K–12 education funding. Funding for major elementary and secondary education programs increased by one-third in just the first three years of NCLB. In FY [fiscal year] 2006, states and local schools will receive $23.3 billion in federal elementary and secondary education aid. Funding for Title I, the primary funding stream in NCLB, has increased to historic levels as well. In fact, because of NCLB, Title I received a larger increase during the first two years of President George W. Bush's administration alone than it did during the previous eight years combined under President Bill Clinton.

Republicans have increased education spending by 150 percent. Since Republicans took control of Congress . . . federal education funding has increased significantly. Funding for the U.S. Department of Education has increased by 150 percent under GOP [Republican] control of the House, from $23 billion in FY 1996 to nearly $58 billion in FY 2006. In fact, the federal government has increased federal education funding so rapidly that states are having trouble spending it all.

A well-funded opportunity—not an unfunded mandate. Education reform opponents have incorrectly claimed that NCLB is an "unfunded mandate." As Brian Riedl of the Heritage Foundation noted in a column [in 2006], NCLB is neither "unfunded" nor a "mandate." States are under no obligation to accept the billions of dollars a year in federal education aid NCLB offers. States that do not wish to be held accountable for improving student achievement, or that prefer to do things their own way, can simply decline the money. In addition, three recent reports conclude the federal government is providing states with more than enough aid to implement the reforms included in NCLB. Information on each report is included below.

Not an Unfunded Mandate

A report from the nonpartisan GAO [Government Accountability Office], requested by Sen. George Voinovich (R-OH) and released in the 108th Congress, upholds Republican claims that the No Child Left Behind Act is not an unfunded mandate. The GAO reviewed more than 500 different statutes and regulations enacted in 2001 and 2002, including Congressional Budget Office (CBO) reports about NCLB, and concluded NCLB was not an unfunded mandate.

According to the report, NCLB "did not meet the UMRA's [Unfunded Mandates Reform Act of 1995] definition of a mandate because the requirements were a condition of federal financial assistance" and "any costs incurred by state, local or tribal governments would result from complying" with conditions of receiving the federal funds.

NCLB May Be Overfunded

A report published in the Spring 2004 edition of the policy journal *Education Next* by two Massachusetts state officials (state board of education chairman James Peyser and chief economist Robert Costrell) concluded the federal government "overshot the target" in terms of funding the law, providing more money than some states need to make it work.

Reform opponents are exaggerating NCLB costs. Peyser and Costrell conclude the increased federal aid states are receiving as a result of the No Child Left Behind law should cover the costs of the additional reforms required. They also concluded "many critics greatly exaggerate the shortfall of federal resources" needed to implement the law's reforms.

Federal spending has "overshot the target." "If this spending increase does not fully cover the fiscal gap [associated with No Child Left Behind's requirements], it would appear to come pretty close—especially when combined with state-level spending increases already required under various state laws and court decisions," Peyser and Costrell wrote. "Given that many states have been slow to implement the statewide assessment and accountability systems required by NCLB, one might even argue that in some instances federal spending growth has overshot the target."

NCLB costs are sufficiently covered. Total federal spending for K–12 education grew significantly from 2001 to 2003 as a result of No Child Left Behind, Peyser and Costrell note, resulting in an $8 billion funding increase that is sufficient—if not more than sufficient—to allow states to meet NCLB's current expectations. The authors say federal education spending must continue to increase in coming years to ensure states continue to have adequate funding to meet NCLB's objectives, but find the actual amount needed is far below the huge amounts claimed by education reform opponents in many states. Additionally, Peyser and Costrell find the $391 million currently appropriated by Congress for states to design and implement annual tests for students in grades 3–8 is adequate at the present time—a conclusion also reached by the independent General Accounting [now "Accountability"] Office (GAO). Five states had already met the NCLB testing requirements before the law even went into effect, they note.

States Profiting Financially

A major national cost study released in February 2004 by Accountability Works, a non-profit research organization, shows states are profiting handsomely from the education spending increases triggered by NCLB.

"Unfunded mandate" claim false. "[W]e conclude that the charge that NCLB is an 'unfunded mandate' is false; additionally, we find that the level of federal funding provided to support implementation of NCLB requirements has been— and is likely to remain—sufficient," the study's authors write.

States will receive $787 million surplus this year from NCLB. The authors' analysis estimates states were to collectively receive a surplus of $787 million in federal No Child Left Behind funding for the (2004–05) school year, a surplus that could increase to $5 billion by the 2007–08 school year. The report also recognizes states are under no obligation to accept the federal education funds that accompany the No Child Left Behind requirements, and cautions against attempts to attribute costs to NCLB that the law does not impose.

States bill feds for their own choices. "States choosing to accept Title I and other federal dollars should be assured that substantial federal resources accompany new demands," the authors note. "There is, however, no reason to assume that the fundamental federal role has changed to the point that all new future K–12 needs are now the responsibility of the federal government."

2

No Child Left Behind Is Closing the Achievement Gap

Margaret Spellings

Margaret Spellings is the United States secretary of education.

According to the results of the Nation's Long-Term Report Card and individual state assessments, No Child Left Behind (NCLB) is working to close the achievement gaps among students across a variety of classifications. Although improvements are needed in the education standards set for high school students, evidence of success among elementary and middle school students is irrefutable. Guidelines are being changed to accommodate the needs of children with disabilities and second-language learners and to account for student growth as a part of achievement. Recent polls make clear that the majority of Americans want to see the standards set by NCLB implemented and achieved.

For all of us in education, the fall is about choosing priorities and setting goals. When Congress overwhelmingly passed No Child Left Behind (NCLB) a few years ago, we set the most ambitious—yet attainable—goal in the history of American education: closing the achievement gap by 2013–2014. In the spirit of the American Dream, we became the first country ever to make a commitment to provide every child with a quality education.

As our students settle into the school year, we are encouraged by strong evidence that NCLB is working. We've also learned that not only is NCLB good policy, it's also good politics.

Report Card Results

Something exciting is going on in America's public schools. We're seeing all-time records set in student learning. The achievement gap is finally closing. Here are just some of the strong signs that NCLB is working:

Nationally, reading scores for 9-year-olds increased more [from 2002 to 2007] than in all the years between 1971 and 1999 combined. African-American and Hispanic students posted some of the biggest gains.

- In math, scores for 9- and 13-year-olds also reached all-time highs. Hispanic 9-year-olds saw their scores rise by 17 points over the [period 2002–07].

- Both 9- and 13-year-olds are reading more than they used to—more than 20 pages a day. Younger students are achieving historically high scores in reading and the achievement gap is narrowing.

- Between white and African-American 9-year-olds, the achievement gap in reading is the smallest ever.

These results are from the Nation's Long-Term Report Card, which was released in July [2007]. The Report Card lets parents, educators and policy-makers check on the quality of America's schools. Its standards and content are set by a bi-partisan group from throughout the education community.

State Assessments

The Report Card's results are above reproach. They clearly show that we're moving in the right direction. In addition to the national Report Card gains, we're seeing terrific progress on state assessments.

- In Georgia, 75 percent of third-grade, English-language learners scored proficient or better in reading, up 23 percentage points from 2002. And, 81 percent of third-grade students with disabilities scored proficient or better in reading, up 26 percentage points from 2002.

- In Wisconsin, 87 percent of third-graders were reading at grade-level or above. This number was an all-time high, and a 13 percent increase over 2002 scores.

- In Maryland, the achievement gaps in reading and math between white and African-American students, and between white and Hispanic students are narrowing. Over the [period 2005–07], 16 percent more African-American third-graders have become proficient in math. And 24 percent more Hispanic third-graders have become proficient in reading.

We're seeing terrific progress because we're challenging what President [George W.] Bush calls "the soft bigotry of low expectations." Before NCLB, student achievement was measured in averages. If most students were performing really well, it was acceptable for others to fail. Many of those were minority children, impoverished children and children with special needs. They were lost in the numbers. They were left behind. But not anymore.

Quite simply, what gets measured gets done.

The Nation's Report Card results prove the fundamental belief underlying NCLB: that every child can learn. Thanks to the hard work of parents, teachers, principals, and state, local and national policy-makers, we can see that all children are capable of tremendous improvement when our schools believe in them and hold them to high standards.

Some Improvement Is Needed

We're pleased with these results, but not satisfied. The latest Long-Term Report Card also shows that our high school students didn't show anywhere near the progress made by students in elementary and middle schools. In fact, Report Card grades for high-school students have barely changed in the last 30 years. We haven't demanded success for older children as we have for younger ones. So high-school students are getting left behind. We clearly must take high standards and accountability into our high schools. We must support older students with the same can-do attitude that helped their younger brothers and sisters. With research-based strategies and policies, we can help older children learn more too. They deserve the same promise of achievement we made [in 2004] for the younger students.

Overall, I found hope in the latest Report Card, but I know we can do better. We are moving in the right direction, but the challenge before us is to stay the course. We can clearly see that NCLB is working with its focus on children in the earlier grades, but we have to continue to be smart about the way the law is executed on the ground.

When it comes to the implementation of NCLB, we are taking a common-sense approach—more outcome-oriented and less bureaucratic—allowing states flexibility where possible and necessary. But this approach is conditioned on one overriding factor: ensuring that real annual progress is made toward getting every single child to read and do math at grade level. The only way to achieve that goal is to adhere to the law's "bright lines" of annual testing and the breakdown of data by student subgroups. Without that information, parents will not know how their children are doing, and educators will not know what to adjust to best help their students. Quite simply, what gets measured gets done.

Common Questions

When I travel around the country, I consistently hear three questions about how we are implementing NCLB.

- How can we best assess students with disabilities?

- Is there a way to give credit to schools for growth in student achievement?

- What should we expect from students who come to the United States with little education and no English fluency?

First, we are continuing to use our best research to make sure children in special education programs are learning and taking tests that are meaningful to them. New research tells us there are students with disabilities who need additional time and intensive instruction to reach grade level. Accordingly, we will be working with states that want to develop "modified tests." So far, 36 states have signed on to this effort by making changes to their accountability plans and committing to develop modified tests for these students—representing about 2 percent of the total student population. We will continue to help states help these children learn.

The Department of Education is also considering the idea of a growth model, which would allow schools to get credit for student progress over time. But I must be clear—to have a sound growth model system, you must have annual data. And, students must be making progress that leads to proficiency as required by law.

We also convened a special working group that discussed how to best measure the progress of children who have not grown up speaking English. We want them to learn the language and meet the same high expectations that we have for all students. The working group included researchers, practitioners and educators who will soon provide recommendations for how to achieve those goals.

That does not mean I'm here to tell states or school districts how to do their jobs. Education policy is primarily a state and local issue. I learned that well during my time with the Texas Legislature. The federal education role has always been to complement states' efforts. The federal government is an 8 percent investor in education and those dollars are targeted towards our neediest children. That's why the Elementary and Secondary Education Act was passed 40 years ago—to help the children who need it most. The bright line principles of NCLB keep us focused on that goal.

NCLB is a partnership, not a mandate. It's an agreement that says if you take federal taxpayer dollars for education you must accept responsibility for increasing student achievement. It also provides historic levels of resources to support schools that are working hard to help students learn. And, it gives parents more information and more choices than they've ever had before—like free after-school tutors and the opportunity to try a new school if their current school is in need of improvement.

We now have signs that [high standards and accountability] really are helping students achieve their dreams.

Good Policy *and* Good Politics

Behind the impressive Nation's Report Card results are tens of thousands of children and families who are depending on us to give them the opportunity that comes with a quality education. When asked, Americans have said they view education as a value, not an issue. People throughout the country—and especially women with children, Hispanics, Catholics and Independents—have said this value is a driving motivation for them.

There is a difference between a value and an issue. Values represent the hopes and dreams that parents have for their children. A value is a lasting belief we hold close to our hearts. It is a principle, a standard and a quality that is worthwhile and desirable. The majority of adults in our country say that a high-quality, public education system is the most important factor in our country's global success. They know education is a fundamental part of our nation's legacy of innovation and achievement. For most people, the very notion of the American Dream starts with getting a quality education.

Virtually every person in our country has a stake in educational achievement. More than one-quarter of all Americans are now enrolled in school—that's almost 75 million people, according to Census Bureau statistics. And that's not even counting the parents and grandparents of children in school.

When we talk about the values inherent in NCLB, our message resonates across the country. In the eight months preceding January 2002, when NCLB became law, support for the Republican Party's stance on education jumped an impressive 25 points.

More than three-quarters of Americans believe that if our high schools don't change soon, our country will be less able to compete in the global marketplace. And almost as many favor extending the law by asking states to set standards for high schools and to make sure that those standards are met. Almost half of minority parents strongly favor this approach—which is almost exactly the percentage of Republicans who strongly favor it. That's the kind of alliance I hope to see a lot more of.

All these people agree on reform because they all know that education is the key to achievement. Millions and millions of Americans of every color and every background—people from every one of our 50 states—trust our public schools with their children. They also trust us with their hopes and dreams for their children's futures. High standards and accountability make a lot of sense to these people, and for good reasons. We now have signs that those concepts really are helping students achieve their dreams.

3

No Child Left Behind Is Not Closing the Achievement Gap

Monty Neill

Monty Neill is executive director of FairTest: the National Center for Fair and Open Testing, located in Cambridge, Massachusetts, and is the author of Implementing Performance Assessments: A Guide to Classroom, School and System Reform *and* Testing Our Children: A Report Card on State Assessment Systems.

The No Child Left Behind Act (NCLB) is obviously failing the nation's children, especially low-income students, the group the law was supposed to help the most. Therefore, NCLB is in need of great revision before it is reauthorized by Congress. Such reform should focus on moving away from excessive testing and school sanctions and toward school improvement, using multiple forms of evidence for school success and local decision making. Although a consensus about the state and goals of the nation's education system used to exist, it is weakening as the persistence of the achievement gap becomes more obvious.

The federal law that is wreaking havoc on educational quality across the nation, No Child Left Behind (NCLB), is due for reauthorization by Congress in 2007. While many observers believe this will not be completed until after the 2008 presidential election[1], we need to begin mobilizing now to ensure that the next version of the longstanding Elementary and Secondary Education Act (ESEA) is a very different law in several critical regards.

1. As of January 2008, the NCLB had not been reauthorized.

Monty Neill, "Overhauling NCLB," *Rethinking Schools Online*, Fall 2006. Reproduced by permission.

The importance of changing the law can scarcely be over-emphasized. While state laws and district practices have often promoted the same harmful policies as NCLB, the federal law has made such programs more onerous, adding more testing and layers of counterproductive "accountability" mandates. And NCLB has made it harder and less likely for states or districts to implement improved assessment and genuine school improvement programs. Over-hauling NCLB should be a political priority, not only for groups working at the national level, but also for local and state individuals and organizations, many of whom have potentially powerful ways to reach out to and influence members of Congress.

To ensure that the new ESEA provides positive assistance to low-income children and their schools, three key things are necessary: a clear, widely agreed-upon vision of what the law should be; an aroused, mobilized, and organized force to support change; and an understanding of the various positions in Congress and what it will take to produce major changes in the law. Each of these points could easily be a separate article, but after short comments on the first two points, I will focus on the third.

Five Guiding Principles

Five principles should guide thinking about a new law.

First, the goal should be high-quality teaching and learning to benefit the whole child, not drill-and-kill to artificially inflate scores on mostly multiple-choice tests in a few subjects.

Second, a new law should focus on the capacity of schools to improve, including adequate resources, professional development, and stronger parental involvement.

Third, any accountability structure must use multiple forms of evidence as the basis for making decisions, not just scores on standardized tests.

Fourth, sanctions must be a last resort and tailored to meet specific problems, not arbitrary actions using one-size-fits-all formulas. They should also be designed to build capacity for improvement, not to punish schools and districts.

Fifth, the new law should effectively empower educators, parents, and communities to work together collaboratively, rather than move decision-making responsibilities ever further from local communities. It should also include equity and civil rights protections to ensure that local empowerment does not mean the power to ignore low-income, racial minority, English-language learning, or disabled children.

The "Joint Organizational Statement on NCLB," signed by 90 national education, civil rights, and religious organizations, outlines key components of what the new ESEA should include. The Forum on Educational Accountability is carrying on this work by developing more detailed proposals on capacity building, assessment, and accountability and by facilitating collaborative action among dozens of groups.

National groups will need to effectively mobilize their constituents to persuade members of Congress to revamp NCLB. This education and pressure could take multiple forms, as suggested in FairTest's "Seven Ways to Work to Overhaul the Federal Education Law," including holding public forums, passing resolutions, writing letters and op-eds, and meeting with members of Congress and state legislators.

Examining the Consensus

For a mobilized constituency to persuade Congress to pass a beneficial education law, it is vital to consider the thinking that underlay passage of NCLB in order to demonstrate that NCLB is not meeting its own goals. (After all, the main stated NCLB goal is a good one: "Ensure that all children have a fair, equal, and significant opportunity to obtain a high-quality education.") It is also necessary to grasp the varying views of NCLB supporters in order to respond, where possible, to their needs, or to counter and isolate proposals that are harmful.

(Among other things, proposals to expand testing, intensify sanctions, develop a national test, and promote privatization are likely.)

Two prominent, pro-NCLB conservative analysts, Frederick Hess and Michael Petrilli, have argued that since the late 1980s, presidents (Clinton and both Bushes) and Congress have forged a "Washington consensus" that revolves around three agreements:

> First, that the nation's foremost education objective should be closing racial and economic achievement gaps. Second, that excellent schools can overcome the challenges of poverty. And third, that external pressure and tough accountability are critical components of helping school systems improve.

This "consensus" sidesteps some major issues such as privatization while ignoring the harmful educational consequences of cheap, test-driven "reform" and ever-more-distant bureaucratic control over schools. However, because this consensus does exist in part, it is a useful tool for thinking about the "bipartisan" agreement supporting NLCB.

[Members of the black and Hispanic caucuses in the House] don't believe high-stakes testing . . . leads to fair outcomes or improved schools.

Hess and Petrilli argue that despite some strong opposition and very thin support among the public and especially among educators, this consensus is likely to hold in Congress. But they also worry that the consensus could fall apart: Bush is weakening, and Republican Congressional leadership has changed while the most conservative Republicans are balking at the intrusiveness of the law as well as its funding requirements. They conclude that the law's survival may depend on

Democrats, especially Sen. Ted Kennedy and Rep. George Miller, who helped craft NCLB and remain as party leaders of the relevant committees.

Historically, as the "Washington consensus" on education evolved, members of the black and Hispanic caucuses in the House opposed both a national test and much of NCLB. They don't believe high-stakes testing, for example, leads to fair outcomes or improved schools. As NCLB was being considered in the House, white liberals and some conservative Republicans joined these caucus members in promoting amendments—such as eliminating the requirement to test in every grade 3–8—that would have made NCLB far less onerous. Though support for such amendments was gaining quickly, time ran out.

Historical analysis suggests that pressure to change the law in fundamental ways will come from both the right and the left. Progressive educators are not likely to have much impact on Republicans, but could—in alliance with mainstream education, civil rights, and other groups—develop a push to change the views of key Democrats.

It is the white liberals who may be pivotal. Like Kennedy and Miller, many believe NCLB is a step forward in civil rights, though they decry the refusal of the Republicans to fully fund the law. Evidence to show the law is not working as they intended, pressure from civil rights groups, and strong alternatives could move more members of Congress toward different legislation.

What About the Gap?

It's time to dismantle the intellectual and evidentiary underpinnings of the "Washington consensus." The political heart of NCLB is its professed goal of closing racial and economic achievement gaps. Bush successfully marshaled rhetoric such as "the soft bigotry of low expectations" and "which child would you leave behind?" to support NCLB and present Republicans as favoring equity. Meanwhile, many Democrats, led by Bill Clinton and many governors and members of Congress, accepted and promoted the unproven notion that standards-based, test-driven accountability would improve schools serving low-income children.

But the test-and-punish structure in NCLB will not overcome the systemic inequities of race and class, the real "gap." While promoting educational equity is essential and should be the central focus of federal support, real progress will require more money and a shift away from the mania for "accountability." The truth is that test-based accountability for schools is not effective at closing real opportunity and learning gaps.

It is becoming increasingly clear that the focus on high-stakes testing is an educational failure.

Despite supporters' claims that NCLB has led to tangible progress, results on the National Assessment of Educational Progress (NAEP) suggest only modest closure of score gaps in some subjects and grades and no change in others. As Jaekyung Lee of the Harvard Civil Rights Project has pointed out, racial gaps closed substantially for younger children from the 1970s into the late 1980s, mostly likely because of policies that attacked racism and poverty. As federal policy retreated from equity concerns, however, one result was that the score gaps widened. They began to close again in the late 1990s— but still not for high school students.

The primary narrowing has been in math. This is due to an intensified emphasis on math instruction. However, as educators are pressured to teach to state tests, NAEP gains appear to be mainly in rote learning, not conceptual understanding or problem-solving.

The price of the focus on accountability testing has been narrowed instruction in the tested subjects and increased focus on rote learning—what [educator and author] Jonathan

Kozol has termed "cognitive decapitation." It has also led to reduced instruction in history, art, and other subjects not included on high-stakes tests.

With no gains in NAEP at grade 12 for any racial group, with independent studies showing that high-stakes tests—including state graduation exams—don't produce improved learning results but do increase dropout rates, it is becoming increasingly clear that the focus on high-stakes testing is an educational failure.

Schools Cannot Work Alone

This Democrat-Republican alliance not only created the "Washington consensus" on testing, it fostered a public discussion in which schools are scapegoated. Congress must be challenged over the notion that schools alone can overcome the effects of racism and poverty. Reports by influential groups such as Education Trust claiming to have identified thousands of "high flying" schools—ones in which low-income kids score high—are misleading. Yes, there are many excellent schools and great educators accomplishing great things with low-income children. But as Designs for Change [a national multiracial, educational research and reform organization] pointed out in a recent study of Chicago, echoing the work of educators such as Deborah Meier and Ann Cook, they do not succeed by turning their schools into test-prep programs.

We should learn from truly good schools. But if the federal government was serious about leaving no child behind, it would address low wages and unemployment; lack of good housing, medical care, and nutrition; community instability; and segregation by race and class. Because schools do have an important role to play, Congress should craft policies that put reasonable expectations on educational systems. Then it should focus support on strengthening beneficial practices to help schools meet them.

In the absence of rational policies and adequate funding to actually improve schools, the idea that "tough accountability" will induce sustained improvement is at best misguided and at worst a deliberate game to undermine educational quality, particularly for low-income children, and privatize public schooling.

Educators and activists must explain to those members of Congress willing to listen why NCLB cannot lead to equitable, high-quality education for all. They need to use emerging proposals to promote a strong, beneficial partnership among the levels of government. They need to engage in extensive public education and mobilization. And they need to create conditions in which those members of Congress who are not willing to consider reason and evidence understand that their tenure in office will be put at risk.

4

Adequate Yearly Progress Reports Are a Hindrance to Educational Success

American Federation of Teachers

Founded in 1916 as a union to represent classroom teachers, the American Federation of Teachers (AFT) has since joined the American Federation of Labor and Congress of Industrial Organizations (AFL-CIO) and expanded its support to include other school-related personnel, government employees, higher education faculty and staff, and nursing and health-care workers.

The Adequate Yearly Progress (AYP) reports required by the No Child Left Behind Act (NCLB) do not effectively measure school or student academic progress. Because succeeding or failing AYP can be influenced by a wide range of nonacademic factors, such as school size, grades tested, and the size and number of NCLB-defined subgroups, AYP provides only a narrow view of accountability. Most schools will inevitably fail AYP regardless of their effectiveness because AYP is a flawed measurement tool that does not take established facts and statistical laws into consideration.

Although the P in AYP [Adequate Yearly Progress] stands for "progress," AYP does not measure progress.[1]

AYP does not measure the *same* students over time (e.g., from one grade to the next or even at the beginning and then

1. AYP reports are used to assess annual school achievement for students in communication arts and math as well as several subgroups based on race, ability, and socioeconomic status. AYP reports are used to ensure that schools are adequately working towards helping all students become proficient by 2014, as mandated by NCLB.

American Federation of Teachers, "What's Wrong with NCLB's AYP Formula? A Summary of Internal and External Research Findings," www.aft.org, 2005. Reproduced by permission.

at the end of the school year), so it is not a *progress* measure at all. Instead, it measures the achievement *status* of *different groups* (cohorts) of students at one point in time in any given year (e.g., the percentage of last year's fourth-graders who hit at least the proficient cut score on the state's tests, the percentage of this year's fourth-graders who did so, next year's percentage, and so on). AYP does not even tell you where these different groups started but only where they ended, and then only in terms of the percentage that made it to the proficient level. . . .

The P in AYP only means the progressively higher state AYP targets a school has to meet, regardless of whether any given cohort of its students started well above or well below the annual, or even the starting, state AYP targets.

Because AYP does not measure progress, it cannot discern whether or not a school has the requisite annual percentage of proficient students because of where its students started—an invalid basis for accountability—or because of its effectiveness in improving achievement, the only valid and fair basis for accountability. . . .

AYP Selectively Measures Accountability

Although NCLB aims to hold *all* schools accountable, AYP only does so selectively. Making or failing AYP (and Safe Harbor) is strongly influenced by a number of non-academic factors, such as a school's size, the number of its grades that are tested by the state, and the size and number of its subgroups—not to mention the laws of statistics.

Larger schools and/or schools with more state-tested grades are more likely to have a subgroup whose size is large enough to count separately in AYP. If School A has a counted subgroup, but School B's identical subgroup is not large enough to count in AYP—and both schools have average proficiency levels that meet the state's AYP targets—School A will fail AYP if its subgroup does, while School B will not, even if its subgroup students score lower than the subgroup in School A.

On average, special education students score very low on regular tests. Therefore, when a school has an AYP-counted special education subgroup, it almost invariably fails AYP— *even when its special education subgroup scores higher than special education students in a school where that subgroup is not large enough to count in AYP.* In Pennsylvania, schools with an AYP-counted special ed subgroup had a 97 percent AYP failure rate; in Massachusetts, the comparable figure was 65 percent; in Maryland, 56 percent; and in New Hampshire, 57 percent.

The more subgroups a school has, the lower its odds of making AYP—not only because subgroup proficiency levels, on average, were below state AYP targets to begin with, but also because it is *statistically* harder for multi-subgroup schools to make AYP than it is for schools with fewer or no AYP-counted subgroups, *even when their average achievement is the same.* In Ohio, schools with more than one subgroup were five times as likely to miss AYP targets as one-subgroup schools (the one usually being a white subgroup). Pennsylvania schools with more than one subgroup were at least three times more likely to fail AYP as one-subgroup schools. In Maryland and Massachusetts, multi-subgroup schools were four times more likely to fail.

Sooner or later, virtually every public school district will fail AYP, but not necessarily because they are 'failures.'

In some states, small schools fell outside of AYP accountability altogether. In most states in 2002–03, entire schools— typically larger ones—were judged on their "effectiveness," including receiving sanctions, based on AYP calculations for students in only one, and sometimes two, of their grades. Under NCLB, no state may hold private schools that receive Title I funds accountable; but every state must apply AYP to *all* of its public schools, even those that do not get Title I funds. The law holds K–2 (untested grades) "feeder schools" accountable for their receiving schools' percentage of proficient students and test-participation rate. . . .

Nearly All Schools Will Fail

Although the A in AYP stands for "adequate," AYP is calculated on the basis of a 100 percent proficiency goal that demands unnatural rates of "progress" from some schools and groups of students, while tolerating inadequate progress or declines among other schools and groups of students—at least for a while. Sooner or later, virtually every public school district and school will fail AYP, but not necessarily because they are "failures."

On average, while achievement levels in disadvantaged schools are much lower than in other schools, their growth rates are the same. Therefore, schools that started substantially below even the state's starting AYP targets—the ones enrolling the most disadvantaged children—must increase their percentage of proficient students at a rate so phenomenal that it has never been reliably evidenced. Conversely, schools that started comfortably above the targets can coast or decline and still make AYP, at least for a while. Ultimately, most schools will fail AYP.

AYP works in a way that treats advantaged and disadvantaged schools, and selective (e.g., magnets) and non-selective schools alike, as if their students all started from the same level of achievement on the day NCLB was signed into law. AYP is also indifferent to the ironclad fact that disadvantaged youngsters, on average, are significantly behind other children before formal schooling even begins.

Even with an acceleration of past rates of progress, the goal of 100 percent proficiency will not be reached by 2014.

Although schools enrolling large numbers of disadvantaged students, followed by large secondary schools, already fail AYP at high rates (and will likely fail many times), nearly all schools will eventually fail AYP. All but the smallest school districts will soon fail. Even though many states changed their implementation of AYP in 2003–04, these changes will only delay the inevitable failure of most schools. This is not because public education is broken or American children are deficient; it is because AYP is unrealistic, does not understand student achievement growth patterns, and does not recognize the laws of statistics.

Although the goal of 100 percent proficiency applies nationally, the states' widely (and wildly) divergent AYP failure rates tell you nothing about the relative achievement or effectiveness of their respective public schools.

Although NCLB stands for 'No Child Left Behind,' AYP leaves many a child behind.

In the first year of AYP implementation, states' AYP failure rates ranged from 7 percent to 85 percent. This variability is not related to differences in educational quality among the states. It is explained in some part by differences in the difficulty of states' academic content standards; differences in the type and difficulty of the tests they use; and by differences in where states set the cut point for "proficient" on their tests. It is explained in even larger part by differences in states' subgroups; differences in school size; differences in the number of grades they test; differences in the number they set for the size a subgroup has to reach in order to count separately in AYP ("minimum N"); whether or not the state uses "confidence intervals" in its AYP calculations; and other factors having nothing to do with educational quality. These points are reinforced by external evidence showing that there is no discernible relationship between states' AYP failure rates and their performance and growth on NAEP [National Assessment of Educational Progress tests].

AYP Leaves Children Behind

Although NCLB stands for "No Child Left Behind," AYP leaves many a child behind.

AYP is indifferent to the achievement of subgroup students in schools with subgroups that are too small to count for AYP, except insofar as their achievement affects the school's average. In Pennsylvania, for example, only 10 percent of schools had an AYP-counted special education subgroup, and in Ohio, less than 1 percent of elementary schools had this subgroup count in AYP. Native American and multi-racial subgroups hardly ever count in AYP.

AYP is indifferent to the achievement of individual and subgroup students at any level or progression of performance other than the proficient level (although Colorado, Massachusetts, Minnesota, and New Hampshire have been allowed to give non-proficient students partial credit). Nor does AYP register declines or stagnations in achievement across and within performance levels, unless they are large enough to affect the schoolwide and/or subgroup percentage of proficient students relative to the annual AYP targets.

There is no reliable evidence that even highly effective schools can produce the huge gains that are necessary for the lowest scoring students to reach AYP's escalating proficiency targets. In Pennsylvania, for example, special education subgroups had an average rating in math of 14.4 percent proficient compared to 54.9 percent for all students. In Maryland, special education subgroups had an average rating in math of 27 percent proficient compared to 50 percent for all students. Conversely, AYP implicitly signals that little or no effort needs to be made with students who are already proficient or above—or in subgroups that are not large enough to count for AYP—because AYP hardly registers them. Therefore, AYP implicitly sets up a perverse set of incentives for schools to concentrate only on raising the scores of students who are just below the proficient cut points on state tests; hard work with other groups is either futile or irrelevant in making AYP.

AYP Does Not Reflect Effectiveness

Since neither the A nor the P in AYP means what it says, it should not be surprising that whether or not a school makes AYP does not necessarily depend on its effectiveness.

There is no discernible relationship between school or subgroup progress and making or failing AYP.

There is no discernible relationship between school or subgroup progress and making or failing AYP. It is where a school or subgroup starts out, relative to the state's annual AYP targets, that counts.

Average and subgroup achievement *growth* is often as great, or greater, in schools that failed AYP as it is in those that made AYP. Average and subgroup growth in a state's AYP-failed schools also tends to meet or exceed the state's average growth rate. In Massachusetts, for example, schools with black, Hispanic or limited English proficient (LEP) subgroups large enough to count separately in AYP determination failed AYP at rates exceeding 80 percent. Yet schools enrolling these subgroups showed greater improvement in the state's composite proficiency index scores than the state average.

Many schools that fail AYP are considerably more successful at making progress with their low-average- and high-scoring students—*all* their students—than are schools that make AYP. Many schools that fail AYP are better at improving low-scoring students' achievement, in particular, than are schools that make AYP, even though schools failing AYP typically have much higher concentrations of poor children than schools that make AYP.

Schools with special education or LEP subgroups large enough to count separately in AYP almost invariably fail AYP—even when the achievement of these subgroup students, as well as their schools as a whole, equals or exceeds that of their peers in schools where these subgroups are too small to be separately counted in AYP.

Although AYP cannot measure school effectiveness, it automatically deems schools that enroll large numbers of special education and low-achieving disadvantaged students "ineffective," regardless of the progress they make with their students.

NCLB rightfully seeks to evaluate and hold schools accountable for their educational effectiveness. But the evidence shows that AYP is an unreliable and invalid measure of effectiveness that holds schools more accountable for where students start than for their academic progress and, in the case of the most disadvantaged schools, for performing an educational feat that has never been reliably evidenced.

5

Testing Is a Crucial Part of Measuring Educational Accountability

Rod Paige

Rod Paige served as U.S. secretary of education from 2001 until his resignation in 2005. He now serves on the board of directors of the News Corporation, an international media conglomerate.

Accountability is essential to the success of any educational endeavor. It is only through testing and the collecting of test data that the system can be proven effective or not. Without such objective measures, students, teachers, and schools fall through the cracks. By helping educators discover students' needs and then measure the effectiveness of their teaching methods in meeting those needs, the assessment tools implemented under No Child Left Behind (NCLB) will ensure that all students are receiving the best education possible. Evidence of the success of NCLB's testing policies abounds nationwide.

Testing is a part of life. In fact, testing starts at the beginning stages of life: The moment we are born, neonatologists measure our reflexes and responses and give us what is called an Apgar score on a scale of one to 10. As we grow up, our teachers test us in school, and we take other standardized tests that compare us with the rest of the nation's students. We are tested if we want to practice a trade, whether it be to

Rod Paige, "Are the Tests Required by No Child Left Behind Making Schools More Accountable? Yes: Testing has Raised Students' Expectations, and Progress in Learning Is Evident Nationwide," *Insight on the News*, May 11, 2004. Reproduced with permission of *Insight*.

get a cosmetology license, a driver's permit or pilot training. And often we are retested and retested again to show that our skills remain at peak level.

In short, tests exist for a reason. In the case of a doctor, they certify that he or she is capable of practicing medicine. In the case of a teacher, they show that he or she has the knowledge to help children learn a given subject. And in the case of a student, they demonstrate whether a child has indeed learned and understood the lesson or the subject.

At their core, tests are simply tools that subjectively measure things. In education, they are particularly important because they pinpoint where students are doing well and where they need help. In fact, testing has been a part of education since the first child sat behind the first desk. Assessments are an important component of educational accountability; in other words, they tell us whether the system is performing as it should. They diagnose, for the teacher, the parent and the student, any problems so that they can be fixed.

Accountability Is Central to NCLB

Educational accountability is the cornerstone of the No Child Left Behind Act, President George W. Bush's historic initiative that is designed to raise student performance across America. The law embraces a number of commonsense ways to reach that goal: accountability for results, empowering parents with information about school performance and giving them options, more local control, and flexibility to tailor the law to local circumstances.

No Child Left Behind is a revolutionary change, challenging the current educational system and helping it to improve. It aims to challenge the status quo by pushing the educational system into the 21st century so that American students leave school better prepared for higher education or the workforce.

Educational accountability is not a new concept; several states have been instituting accountability reforms for years.

No Child Left Behind builds on the good work of some of these states that were at the forefront of the reform movement. The truth is that this law has one goal: to get all children reading and doing math at grade level. It's that simple. The law itself is a federal law, but it is nothing more than a framework. Elementary and secondary education are the traditional province of state and local governments, which is why the specific standards, tests and most of the other major tenets of the law are designed and implemented by the state departments of education, because they are in the best position to assess local expectations and parental demands.

NCLB focuses on facts, not just feelings and hunches.

The federal role in education also is not a new concept. There is a compelling national interest in education, which is why the federal government is involved and has been for some time. The federal government has stepped in to correct overt unfairness or inequality, starting with measures to enforce civil rights and dismantle segregation in the wake of the *Brown v. Board of Education* case (a Supreme Court decision that is now 50 years old). The federal government's first major legislative involvement in education goes back to 1965 with the Elementary and Secondary Education Act, which marked the first federal aid given to school districts with large percentages of children living in poverty. In 2001 the law was reauthorized as the No Child Left Behind Act (NCLB), which preserves the states' traditional role but asks them to set standards for accountability and teacher quality, thereby improving the quality, inclusivity, fairness and justice of American education.

NCLB focuses on facts, not just feelings and hunches. It is no longer acceptable simply to believe schools are improving without knowing for certain whether they are. As [former U.S. senator from New York] Robert F. Kennedy asked back in 1965 when this federal education law was first debated, "What happened to the children? [How do we know] whether they can read or not?" With new state-accountability systems and tests we will have the full picture.

The Old System Is a Failure

Let's examine what we do know. According to the nation's report card (the National Assessment of Educational Progress, or NAEP), only one in six African-Americans and one in five Hispanics are proficient in reading by the time they are high-school seniors. NAEP math scores are even worse: Only 3 percent of blacks and 4 percent of Hispanics are testing at the proficient level. This is the status quo result of a decades-old education system before the NCLB.

Of the 10 fastest-growing occupations in the United States, the top five are computer-related, which are jobs that require high-level skills. High-school dropouts need not apply. We are all concerned about outsourcing jobs overseas, and we should note that the unemployment rate for high-school dropouts is almost twice that of those with high-school diplomas (7.3 percent compared with 4.2 percent) and nearly four times that of college graduates (7.3 percent vs. 2.3 percent). For young black men the unemployment rate is a staggering 26 percent. Even a high-school diploma isn't the cure: A vast majority of employers sadly expect that a high-school graduate will not write clearly or have even fair math skills. No wonder a recent study claimed a high-school diploma has become nothing more than a "certificate of attendance." For millions of children, they were given a seat in the school but not an education of the mind.

NCLB helps us zero in on student needs.

It is clear that our system as a whole is not preparing the next generation of workers for the global economy ahead of them. As [former] Federal Reserve Chairman Alan Greenspan noted recently: "We need to be forward looking in order to adapt our educational system to the evolving needs of the economy and the realities of our changing society. It is an effort that should not be postponed." That's why I am so passionate about making these historic reforms and drawing attention to the issue.

The old system, the status quo, is one that we must fight to change. That's why the president and both parties in Congress understood the urgency of the situation and put NCLB into law. They also ensured that the money would be there to get the job done, providing the means to states fully to implement the law; indeed, there's been 41 percent more federal support for education since President Bush took office.

Education for All

But some defenders of the status quo have aired complaints about the law, saying its requirements are unreasonable and the tests are arbitrary. The bottom line is, these cynics do not believe in the worth of all children; they have written some of them off. You can guess which ones fall into that category. This pessimism relegates these children to failure. The president aptly refers to this phenomenon as the "soft bigotry of low expectations." But NCLB says the excuses must stop; all children must be given a chance.

NCLB helps us zero in on student needs. With little information about individual students' abilities with different skills, most teachers must rely on a "buckshot" approach to teaching their classes, aiming for the middle and hoping to produce a decent average. With an emphasis on scientifically based research techniques and effective use of information, NCLB helps fund programs that teachers can use to identify specific areas of weakness among their students.

For example, the Granite School District in Utah used Title I funds (support for economically disadvantaged students) to procure the "Yearly Progress Pro" computer program. Now a fourth-grade class at Stansbury Elementary School visits the computer lab for a quick 15-minute test each week; the teacher walks out with a printout identifying changes in performance in specific skill areas over the week.

The Improvements Add Up

Child by child, the improvements add up. For example, a study by the Council of Great City Schools examined the recent gains in large metropolitan school systems. The Beating the Odds IV report showed that since NCLB has been implemented, public-school students across the country have shown a marked improvement in reading. The report found that the achievement gap in reading and math between African-Americans and whites, and Hispanics and whites in large cities, is narrowing for fourth- and eighth-grade students. And it appears, according to the report, that our big-city schools are closing the gap at a faster rate than the statewide rate. Not only are the achievement gaps closing, the report states, but also math and reading achievement are improving.

For a concrete example of how the law is working, look at the Cheltenham School District in Pennsylvania, where leaders are disaggregating data to find the cracks they must fill. Drawing on test results, the district provides schools with specific information about each student's abilities and weaknesses in specific academic areas. Schools receive this data in easily accessible electronic formats in July, before the students arrive, giving them time to plan for the year. Now teachers can account for the effectiveness of their strategies and, if they are not working for some students, adapt to alternatives.

These findings are especially significant because research shows that it is often the students in the large-city schools who need the most help and face the greatest odds. Clearly, this report demonstrates that if you challenge students, they will rise to the occasion. This concept is at the fundamental core of NCLB because we can no longer mask our challenges in the aggregate of our successes. We must make sure that all children, regardless of their skin color and Zip codes, have the opportunity to receive a high-quality education.

While the press focuses on the complaints of the unwilling, whole communities are taking on the challenge of accountability and achieving great results. Perhaps my favorite example is in the Peck School in rural Michigan, where I visited ... and found that the school culture had embraced the accountability treatment. A huge poster hangs in the hallway of the school emblazoned with No Child Left Behind! Showing creativity and commitment, the school launched a tutoring program, began intervening sooner with low-performing students, and even created a peer-counseling program to address the conflicts that often spill into the classroom and distract from learning. Everyone in the Peck School is taking responsibility for the students' education, truly fostering the character of good citizenship.

It is time to think of the children and to give them what they need. It is time to work to make the law successful. We need to create an American public educational system that matches the vision of this law, where we strive for excellence without exclusion, where our children achieve greatness rather than greatly underachieving, and where 10 or 20 years from now a new generation of adults realize that we gave them a better life because we had courage and conviction now.

6

High-Stakes Testing Has a Negative Impact on Learning

David C. Berliner and Sharon L. Nichols

David C. Berliner is an education professor at Arizona State University and a past president of the American Educational Research Association. Sharon L. Nichols is an educational psychology professor at the University of Texas at San Antonio. They are the coauthors of Collateral Damage: How High-Stakes Testing Corrupts America's Schools.

The No Child Left Behind Act (NCLB) focuses on testing as the sole means of measuring academic success. While assessment tools are needed, these high-stakes tests encourage underhanded manipulation of students and test data. In addition, more time is now being spent on test preparation than on authentic teaching and learning, and teachers are beginning to feel that their credibility and value as educators are being compromised for the sake of collecting data that are often not reflective of student, teacher, or school performance. One way of reforming this test-focused system is to implement formative testing that encourages learning as opposed to summative testing that prevents learning. The end result of test-based education may well be a loss of creativity and critical thinking.

In his 2007 State of the Union address, President [George W.] Bush claimed success for the federal No Child Left Behind Act. "Students are performing better in reading and

David C. Berliner and Sharon L. Nichols, "High-Stakes Testing Is Putting the Nation at Risk," As first appeared in *Education Week*, March 12, 2007. Reprinted with permission from the authors.

math, and minority students are closing the achievement gap," he said, calling on Congress to reauthorize this "good law." Apparently, the president sees in No Child Left Behind what he sees in Iraq: evidence that his programs are working. But, as with Iraq, a substantial body of evidence challenges his claim.

We believe that this federal law ... puts American public school students in serious jeopardy. Extensive reviews of empirical and theoretical work, along with conversations with hundreds of educators across the country, have convinced us that if Congress does not act in this session to fundamentally transform the law's accountability provision, young people and their educators will suffer serious and long-term consequences. If the title were not already taken, our thoughts on this subject could be headlined "A Nation at Risk."

We note in passing that only people who have no contact with children could write legislation demanding that *every* child reach a high level of performance in three subjects, thereby denying that individual differences exist. Only those same people could also believe that *all* children would reach high levels of proficiency at precisely the same rate of speed.

Validity problems in the testing of English-language learners and special education students also abound, but we limit our concerns in this essay to the No Child Left Behind law's reliance on high-stakes testing. The stakes are high when students' standardized-test performance results in grade retention or failure to graduate from high school. The stakes are high when teachers and administrators can lose their jobs or, conversely, receive large bonuses for student scores, or when humiliation or praise for teachers and schools occurs in the press as a result of test scores. This federal law requires such high-stakes testing in all states.

Campbell's Law

More than 30 years ago, the eminent social scientist Donald T. Campbell warned about the perils of measuring effectiveness via a single, highly consequential indicator: "The more any quantitative social indicator is used for social decision making," he said, "the more subject it will be to corruption pressures and the more apt it will be to distort and corrupt the social processes it is intended to monitor." High-stakes testing is exactly the kind of process Campbell worried about, since important judgments about student, teacher, and school effectiveness often are based on a single test score. This exaggerated reliance on scores for making judgments creates conditions that promote corruption and distortion. In fact, the overvaluation of this single indicator of school success often compromises the validity of the test scores themselves. Thus, the scores we end up praising and condemning in the press and our legislatures are actually untrustworthy, perhaps even worthless.

Campbell's law is ubiquitous, and shows up in many human endeavors. Businesses, for example, regularly become corrupt as particular indicators are deemed important in judging success or failure. If stock prices are the indicator of a company's success, for example, then companies like Enron, Qwest, Adelphia, and WorldCom manipulate that indicator to make sure they look good. Lives and companies are destroyed as a result. That particular indicator of business success became untrustworthy as both it and the people who worked with it were corrupted.

Similarly, when the number of criminal cases closed is the indicator chosen to judge the success of a police department, two things generally happen: More trials are brought against people who may be innocent or, with a promise of lighter sentences, deals are made with accused criminals to get them to confess to crimes they didn't commit.

When the indicators of success and failure in a profession take on too much value, they invariably are corrupted. Those of us in the academic world know that when researchers are judged primarily by their publication records, they have occasionally fabricated or manipulated data. This is just another instance of Campbell's law in action.

Testing Corrupts Education

We have documented hundreds of examples of the ways in which high-stakes testing corrupts American education in a new book, *Collateral Damage*. Using Campbell's law as a framework, we found examples of administrators and teachers who have cheated on standardized tests. Educators, acting just like other humans do, manipulate the indicators used to judge their success or failure when their reputations, employment, or significant salary bonuses are related to those indicators.

We found examples of administrators who would falsify school test data or force low-scoring students out of school in their quest to avoid public humiliation. We documented the distortion of instructional values when teachers focused on "bubble" kids—those on the cusp of passing the test—at the expense of the education of very low or very high scorers. We found instances where callous disregard for student welfare had replaced compassion and humanity, as when special education students were forced to take a test they had failed five times, or when a student who had recently suffered a death in the family was forced to take the test anyway.

Because so much depends on how students perform on tests, it should not be surprising that, as one Florida superintendent noted, "when a low-performing child walks into a classroom, instead of being seen as a challenge, or an opportunity for improvement, for the first time since I've been in education, teachers are seeing [that child] as a liability." Shouldn't we be concerned about a law that turns too many of the country's most morally admired citizens [teachers] into morally compromised individuals?

We also documented the narrowing of the curriculum to just what is tested, and found a huge increase in time spent in test preparation instead of genuine instruction. We found teachers concerned about their loss of morale, the undercutting of their professionalism, and the problem of disillusionment among their students. Teachers and administrators told us repeatedly how they were not against accountability, but that they were being held responsible for their students' performance regardless of other factors that may affect it. Dentists aren't held responsible for cavities and physicians for the onset of diabetes when youngsters don't brush their teeth, or eat too much junk food, they argue.

Teachers know they stand a better chance of being successful where neighborhoods and families are healthy and communicate a sense of efficacy, where incomes are both steady and adequate, and where health-care and child-care programs exist. So the best of them soon move to schools with easier-to-teach students. This is no way to close the achievement gap.

We are turning America into a nation of test-takers, abandoning our heritage as a nation of thinkers, dreamers, and doers.

Replacing a Flawed System

Dozens of assessment experts have argued eloquently and vehemently that the high-stakes tests accompanying the implementation of the No Child Left Behind Act are psychometrically inadequate for the decisions that must be made about students, teachers, and schools. Furthermore, the testing standards of the American Educational Research Association are being violated in numerous ways by the use of high-stakes tests to comply with the law. The law, therefore, makes all who engage in compliance activities traitors to their own profession. It forces education professionals to ignore the testing standards that they have worked so hard to develop. We wonder, would the federal government treat members of the American Medical Association or the National Academy of Sciences with such disdain?

In reauthorization hearings for the law, members of Congress should abandon high-stakes testing and replace it with an accountability system that is more reasonable and fair.

What might such a system look like?

A move to more "formative" assessments and an abandonment of our heavy commitment to "summative" assessments would be welcome. Assessment *for* learning, as opposed to assessment *of* learning, has produced some impressive gains in student achievement in other countries, and ought to be tried here. Likewise, the use of an inspectorate—an agency that sends expert observers into schools—has proved itself useful in other countries, and could also help improve schools in the United States.

End-of-course exams designed by teachers, as some states are now offering, increase teachers' commitment to the testing program and, if the teachers get to score the tests, can also be a great professional-development opportunity. There are other alternatives to high-stakes testing, as well.

Our research informs us that high-stakes testing is hurting students, teachers, and schools. It is putting the nation at risk. By restricting the education of our young people and substituting for it training for performing well on high-stakes examinations, we are turning America into a nation of test-takers, abandoning our heritage as a nation of thinkers, dreamers, and doers.

7

No Child Left Behind Has Helped English Language Learners

Clemencia Cosentino de Cohen and Beatriz Chu Clewell

Clemencia Cosentino de Cohen is a sociologist and research associate in the Program for Evaluation and Equity Research (PEER) of the Urban Institute, where Beatriz Chu Clewell serves as director and principal research associate. The Urban Institute is a nonprofit, nonpartisan policy research and educational organization that examines social, economic, and governance problems of public interest.

Given that English language learners (ELL) and limited English proficient (LEP) students are the most rapidly growing subgroups in American elementary schools, there is great interest in their achievement, especially in light of No Child Left Behind (NCLB) reforms. Although the adjustment to NCLB protocols has been somewhat problematic for some students in schools with high rates of LEP students, the overall results of these changes have been positive. Not only has NCLB forced schools to devote more attention to ELL students, but the reforms have resulted in improvements in curriculum, teacher preparation, and assessment. In addition, NCLB guidelines have raised the achievement standards for all ELL students.

To expand knowledge about young immigrant populations and to document how the No Child Left Behind Act (NCLB) affects the education of English language learner

Clemencia Cosentino de Cohen and Beatriz Chu Clewell, "Putting English Language Learners on the Educational Map: The No Child Left Behind Act Implemented," *Urban Institute*, May 21, 2007. Reproduced by permission.

(ELL) and limited English proficient (LEP) students, the Urban Institute was funded by the Foundation for Child Development to undertake a series of reports. . . .

This policy brief draws on this work to address the main question guiding the series: *has NCLB improved education for ELLs as schools have become accountable for these students' performance?* . . .

The findings reveal that, while implementation of NCLB in high-LEP schools has resulted in some problems for ELL students' education, the net effect of the law has been positive because it has (a) increased attention paid to ELL students; (b) increased the alignment of curriculum, instruction, professional development, and testing; and (c) raised the bar for ELL student achievement. . . .

English Language Learners

Limited English proficient students are the most rapidly growing population in U.S. elementary schools. Between 1980 and 2000, the share of English language learners in elementary schools increased by over 50 percent, from 4.7 to almost 7.4 percent of all children (or almost two million children). This rising trend should not be surprising given record-high immigration rates over the same period. In 2000, over half of immigrant children in grades pre-K to grade 5 were from Latin America, and one-quarter from Asia. These children add to the growing numbers of English language learners or limited English proficient students educated in the nation's schools. This is particularly true in kindergarten, where LEP students constitute a larger share of students (10 percent) than in other grades (6 to 7 percent).

Limited English proficient students are concentrated in a few states but are spreading rapidly throughout the nation. While five states—California, Texas, New York, Florida, and Illinois—are home to almost 70 percent of all LEP students in elementary school, growth in this student population has been more rapid in other destinations. Between 1990 and 2000, the number and share of LEP students grew most rapidly in states in the Southeast and Midwest. Some states had growth rates above 200 percent (Nevada and Nebraska were at the top with 350 percent growth). This marks an important shift in this population away from traditional receiving states (Florida, New York, and others) in favor of other destinations (such as Arkansas and Georgia).

The majority of LEP elementary school students are concentrated in a small number of schools: nearly 70 percent of the nation's LEP students enroll in only 10 percent of elementary schools. Labeled "high-LEP," in these 5,000 schools LEP students account for almost one-half of the student body (on average), a striking contrast to the 5 percent average of LEP students enrolled in the remaining elementary schools that serve English language learners (called "low-LEP"). Also striking is the fact that nearly half of elementary schools in the United States enroll no limited English proficient students. These findings show that English language learners are highly concentrated in a limited number of schools serving primarily ELL and immigrant students. . . .

After NCLB: Schools Respond

How has NCLB been implemented in high-LEP schools? The following are examples from our case study sites, which included three districts and six high-LEP schools.

There was a great deal of variation in the way districts with high-LEP schools implemented NCLB testing requirements in both subject areas and ELP (English Language Proficiency). These variations are evident in terms of the actual *tests* used, the way *exemptions* are applied, and the use of *accommodations* in testing ELL students. Although all districts used ELP tests in compliance with both Title I and Title III requirements, some used tests inappropriately to measure both subject area and ELP skills. For example, one district used an ELP test, developed to measure English language proficiency only, to assess content area knowledge of ELLs. Another district required that ELL students take the same English language tests in math and language arts that were administered to all students. One of the case study districts allowed no exemptions from testing for NCLB purposes, and the only accommodation provided to these students was the fact that they took a different test. Another district reviewed exemption requests from schools and determined which ELLs should be tested and made suggestions regarding accommodations. A third district exempted ELL students who had been attending school for fewer than three years from the English language arts test and administered a state English proficiency test instead. Testing accommodations allowed by districts ranged from none to a laundry list of several, including small group administration, repeating directions, extending time, reading of a listening section, use of bilingual glossaries, written response in a native language, and simultaneous use of English and an alternative language.

NCLB had a positive effect on the alignment of curriculum, instruction, and assessment in high-LEP case study schools.

NCLB had a positive effect on the alignment of curriculum, instruction, and assessment in high-LEP case study schools. Although the districts in our case studies were at different stages in the alignment process, NCLB seems to have increased their drive to align ELL programs with the general curriculum, state standards, and assessments. All the districts in our study were focused on achieving alignment: one district, where alignment had already been achieved, was adapting content lessons in English language courses for ELL programs, while the other two districts were actively involved in alignment activities and were collaborating with regional consortia to develop new ELP standards aligned with ELP tests. The districts in our study found it difficult to provide school choice to all eligible students, including ELL students. They cite logistical reasons such as overcrowding for their inability to accommodate eligible students for school choice. This did not seem to present a problem, however, because fewer students than were eligible actually opted for school choice. Two factors inhibited the use of the school choice option by parents of ELL students: parental preference for neighborhood schools and reluctance to bus children long distances in order to attend a public school of choice. Additional inhibiting factors included parental trust in the schools that ELL students were attending and a lack of information received by immigrant parents about their school choice options.

The high-LEP school districts in our study all offered Supplemental Educational Services (SES) to eligible students, although lack of data on actual use by eligible ELL students made it difficult to determine their adequacy. All three school districts provided SES, with two districts offering services that were centralized at the district level and the third providing SES mainly through individual schools. Limited information on the use of SES by ELL students prevented a determination of whether students had access to adequate and appropriate SES. Because high-ELL schools, prior to NCLB, were more likely to offer such Title I services as academic support, enrichment, and remedial programs, these schools may have been able to build on previously established support services to fulfill the NCLB requirement for SES.

Professional development was a major mechanism for improving high-LEP schools under NCLB. This has been especially true for schools identified as in need of improvement. Professional development has been used to help teachers align curriculum to state content standards and assessment. It has also been a means by which ESL [English as a second language]/bilingual teachers learned about cutting-edge instructional techniques for ELL students. Bilingual/ESL teachers and general education teachers have also been encouraged to coordinate instruction for ELL students through professional development workshops. Our findings regarding high-LEP schools confirm that both bilingual and general education teachers in these schools report receiving more professional development than do teachers in schools with lower LEP enrollment. In addition, general education teachers in high-LEP schools report receiving training in teaching LEP students.

Parents of ELL students in high-LEP enrollment schools professed to have very little knowledge of the requirements of NCLB. As required by NCLB, the districts and schools in our study conducted considerable parental outreach, mostly consisting of translation and dissemination of basic information about NCLB targeted to parents of ELL students. All schools had adopted a parental involvement policy and used mechanisms for parental outreach, such as parent coordinators, parent volunteer programs, and school-based activities for parents. These efforts notwithstanding, most parents seemed to understand very little about the law. This was attributed by school personnel to parents' low literacy levels and lack of familiarity with the U.S. educational system. Parents of ELL students, who are often recent immigrants, pose a particular challenge because of linguistic, educational, and cultural barriers to communication. Recent data show that a third of children of immigrants in pre-K to 5th grade had parents without high school degrees, compared with only 9 percent of students with native-born parents.

> *Teachers and staff in the high-LEP schools . . . commented that NCLB had raised the bar for ELL student achievement.*

NCLB had an effect on pre-K education at the case study sites. Although NCLB does not directly address pre-K and only 2 percent of NCLB funds are used for pre-K education, there is evidence from our case study data to suggest that NCLB has had a spillover effect on pre-K education. This effect can be seen as an extension of the law's effect on K–5 students. At least in the case study sites, NCLB seems to have raised standards in pre-K education and resulted in a movement toward aligning the pre-K curriculum with district and state standards. An additional effect has been the expansion of teacher and paraprofessional quality requirements to encompass pre-K staff. Because high-LEP schools are more likely to have pre-K programs, this indirect influence of NCLB may have been experienced more widely in these schools.

NCLB Puts ELL Students on the Map

By increasing the accountability of states, districts, and schools for the educational success of ELL students, especially those in high-LEP settings, NCLB has focused attention on the educational needs of this group. A principal of a case study school summed up the general feelings of most district and school personnel in our study: "I think that NCLB has not been a bad thing for LEP students. It's put them on the map, so to speak, because of the increased accountability for their learning." Shining a spotlight on ELL students has resulted in improvement not only of the services provided to these students but also of the educational strategies employed to educate them. This enhanced approach is manifested through

- a new focus on aligning ELL instruction and assessment with state content standards;

- increased emphasis on literacy and math;

- enhanced efforts to train ESL teachers in effective instructional strategies;

- exposure of general classroom teachers to ESL instructional methods;

- increased instructional coordination between ESL/ bilingual teachers and general classroom teachers;

- greater specificity in the prescription of instruction to guide the English language acquisition process; and

- greater awareness of the inadequacy of most English language proficiency assessments.

ELL students are also being held to higher standards. Teachers and staff in the high-LEP schools in our study commented that NCLB had raised the bar for ELL student achievement. An assistant principal observed that ELL students were doing better than they had been a few years earlier because "standards are high." Kindergarten teachers in one of the schools commented that because of NCLB and other district initiatives, "kindergarten now is what first grade used to be." Teachers also spoke of intensifying their efforts to help students learn and of following the curriculum more closely, driven by the need to meet the higher standards demanded by NCLB. Observed one teacher: "My kids are learning more now. It pushes me to teach them more—I know how hard the test is." This increase in expectations seems to have had a spillover effect on pre-K education. Because schools are teaching more advanced material in kindergarten to give students a "head start," it has been necessary to improve pre-K education to ease students' transition into kindergarten and the early years of schooling. Accordingly, in the schools visited, the pre-K curriculum has been aligned with district and state standards, and NCLB requirements for high-quality teachers and paraprofessionals have been expanded to include pre-K staff.

The effects of NCLB on ELL students, nevertheless, have not been wholly positive. District and school personnel repeatedly cite increased testing requirements as having caused undue stress for teachers and students. As described above, testing practices espoused by some high-LEP school districts have hurt rather than helped ELL students. And although the heightened attention to ELL students has benefited those in high-LEP schools, this may not be true for ELL students in low-LEP schools (and districts), as there might not be enough of them to require disaggregation of their scores as a separate group.

The benefits of a critical mass apply to LEP concentration. This study also shows that limited English proficient elementary school students are highly concentrated: 70 percent of them enroll in only 10 percent of our schools. This high degree of concentration—while undoubtedly negative in terms of limiting interaction among native and immigrant students—does make the provision of specialized services more cost-effective and a higher priority, which enhances the likelihood that such services will be offered. It is often easier to justify expenditures for special programs when a large proportion of the student body will benefit. This probably helps explain the evidence presented in this research of the use of approaches and strategies considered effective for this population: standardized identification procedures, remedial and enrichment support programs, and specialized instruction for ELLs, such as bilingual education, foreign language immersion programs, and native language instruction. Post-NCLB, districts and schools with high LEP concentration have been more motivated to improve education for these students because LEP students comprise an identifiable group for which schools are held accountable.

Low-LEP schools may not adequately serve growing numbers of immigrant children spreading throughout the nation. Nearly one-third of all limited English proficient children enroll in schools serving low percentages of LEP students. When NCLB passed, these mostly suburban schools lagged behind high-LEP schools in providing instruction adapted to the needs of LEP children, providing in-service professional development for general education teachers related to teaching LEP students, and offering important student services, such as support and enrichment programs. The documented spread of immigrants to nontraditional locations is causing LEP student enrollment to become more diffuse across schools. As this process of immigrant expansion throughout the nation continues, it will be of particular importance for all schools to offer the services needed to help LEP children succeed. Perhaps a greater emphasis on exposing non-ESL/bilingual teachers to the needs of LEP students through both preservice and in-service training can be a starting point to address this problem. This is important even in schools that have moderate or small LEP populations, where LEP students are isolated (in numbers too small to require that test scores be reported separately under NCLB). Training on LEP education among teachers in these schools would not only help their LEP students, who otherwise run the risk of being overlooked, but would also help teachers prepare for the likely possibility that in the near future, the LEP population at their schools will grow and become a reporting category.

8

Special Education Students Thrive Under No Child Left Behind

Candace Cortiella

Candace Cortiella is director of the Advocacy Institute, a non-profit organization that develops products and services that help improve the lives of persons with disabilities. She is also on the Professional Advisory Board of the National Center for Learning Disabilities, a nonprofit organization that serves as an advocate for children, adolescents, and adults with learning disabilities.

Before the No Child Left Behind Act (NCLB) was signed into law in 2002, special needs students were not given much attention in terms of accountability, even though they were expected to meet the same standards as all other students. Adequate Yearly Progress (AYP) reports and other assessment tools required by NCLB have finally placed much-needed focus on special education students. Although the system is not perfect, data show that the reforms enacted by NCLB are making a difference toward closing the achievement gap.

For one group of students—those who receive special education services—NCLB has provoked discussions that span a wide range of opinions and positions. While much of the impact of NCLB remains to be seen—after all, full implementation only began in the 2005–2006 school year—it's time to take a look at what we know about the rewards and road-blocks for special education students. This report provides a look at several specific requirements of the No Child Left Behind Act (NCLB) and their impact on students receiving special education supports and services.

Who They Are

Almost fourteen percent—some 6.6 million—of this nation's school-age children receive some level of additional support through special education. These children come from all races and ethnic groups and speak many different languages. Significant numbers are served by other school programs, such as Title I and English Language services, in addition to special education. . . .

Special education students are expected to meet the same state educational standards as all other students. The additional assistance of their individualized, specially designed instruction (detailed in an annual commitment of resources known as the Individualized Education Program or IEP) provides the extra support needed to reach such a level of achievement.

Special education classification has too frequently been used to diminish the expectations for the students designated as eligible for such services and to minimize the responsibility of general education teachers and administrators for their progress. Also, data suggests that special education classification is used to segregate minority students, particularly Black boys. Black students represent more than 20 percent of those receiving special education yet make up only 17 percent of public school enrollment. . . .

One aspect of the marginalization of special education students has been the pervasive practice of failing to include these students in the state assessments required of all other students. Despite requirements in both the 1994 version of the ESEA [Elementary and Secondary Education Act]—known as the Improving America's Schools Act—and the 1997 version of the IDEA [Individuals with Disabilities Education Act]—that special education students participate in all state assessments and that the results of their participation be publicly reported, massive exclusion prevailed. Without participation, there is no accountability nor will attention be paid to needed improvements in the achievement of these students.

NCLB's requirement that . . . at least 95 percent of all students [be tested] . . . has finally catapulted special education students into the realm of full accountability.

This systematic exclusion from accountability systems is particularly egregious when examined in the context of the characteristics of the disability categories that make up the population of students receiving special education.

Simply put, the vast majority of students receiving special education in our nation's schools—some 85 percent—are found eligible under a disability category that in no way precludes them from—with appropriate services and supports—functioning at or above grade level or from achieving proficiency on a state's academic content standards in reading and math. . . .

Making Them Matter

NCLB's requirement that schools, school districts and states test at least 95 percent of all students in the required grades and academic areas—and at least 95 percent of each required subgroup—has finally catapulted special education students into the realm of full accountability.

There is no doubt that this participation requirement—part of the trifecta known as "Adequate Yearly Progress" or, simply, "AYP"—has finally motivated states to begin to fully include all students in state assessments, including students receiving special education services. . . .

However, states "ability to fully include all students receiving special education in state assessments continues to be hampered. In its 2006 *National Assessment of Title I Interim Report*, the U.S. Department of Education noted:

> ". . . The lowest participation rates were for students with disabilities. While states missing the test participation requirement for other subgroups often missed by just one or two percentage points, states that failed to assess 95 percent of students with disabilities typically had lower participation rates for those students (as low as 77 percent in one state)."

While participation has seen a dramatic increase due to NCLB's participation requirements, the participation has not always been meaningful. For example, while the percentage of special education students participating in state assessments in Texas increased from 47 percent in 2000–2001 to 99 percent in 2003–2004, more than half of those tested were given an "out of level" test.

Marginal Participation

Out-of-level testing (OOLT) means assessing students enrolled in a specific grade level with tests designed for students at lower grade levels. As such, an OOLT does not measure a student's mastery of grade-level content or achievement standards—a measurement that is key to the school accountability goal of NCLB.

Out-of-level testing is often associated with lower expectations for students receiving special education, tracking these students into lower-level curricula with limited opportunities. It may also limit a student's opportunities for advancing to the next grade or graduating with a regular high school diploma. It also assumes that a student being tested below grade level will automatically recall the content from a past grade. According to the National Center on Educational Outcomes, research does not support the use of out-of-level test scores from state assessments when measuring student proficiency or otherwise on standards for the grade level in which a student is enrolled.

Because an out-of-level assessment fails to measure a student's mastery of grade-level content, states that choose to administer such an assessment must consider it the same as an alternate assessment based on alternate achievement standards for AYP determinations according to NCLB regulations. As such, proficient and advanced scores fall under NCLB's limit of no more than one percent of the scores of all students assessed in the school district or state. This regulatory limitation has provided an important safeguard to what has been an overused assessment practice by states unwilling to develop assessments that can allow students with disabilities to fully demonstrate their knowledge on grade level content.

Moving Them Forward

NCLB's requirement for universal proficiency in reading and math by 2013–2014 has, in the opinion of most, brought about much needed attention to the instruction of students receiving special education. In early 2007, the Commission on No Child Left Behind, a bipartisan, independent commission formed to develop recommendations for the reauthorization of the No Child Left Behind Act, released its final report. In it, the Commission found that

> Overall, we were left with the strong impression that NCLB has resulted in a much higher awareness of and focus on the achievement of students with disabilities. *Source: Beyond NCLB: Fulfilling the Promise to Our Nation's Children, 2007, pg. 67*

In fact, given the long-standing practice of excluding students who are receiving special education services from large-scale assessments—or testing them on content far below their age appropriate grade level—these students can be viewed as performing extraordinarily well.

An examination of seven-year trends of the percentage of elementary special education students who achieved proficiency on statewide reading exams across ten states shows consistent gains in most states.

Five states . . . saw improvements of more than 20 percentage points in the number of special education students achieving proficiency on the state's regular assessment.

Further evidence of performance improvement was provided by the U.S. Department of Education in its 2006 National Assessment of Title I Interim Report, which found that from 2000–2001 to 2002–2003, 14 of 20 states experienced an increase in the percentage of 4th-grade special education students performing at or above the state's proficient level in reading and 16 of 20 states experienced an increase in math. This outpaced the improvements experienced for all other student groups. . . .

Further evidence of improved achievement is provided by extensive analysis done by the National Center on Educational Outcomes (NCEO)—a federally funded center that monitors the participation of special education students in national and state assessments. NCEO analyzed the performance of special education students for 25 states on regular elementary reading assessments for the four years from 2001–2002 through 2004–2005. In 2001–2002, these states had an average proficiency rate of 34 percent. That proficiency rate improved to 43 percent in 2004–2005. Five states—Alaska, Alabama, Kansas, Maryland, and South Dakota, saw improvements of more than 20 percentage points in the number of special education students achieving proficiency on the state's regular assessment—the same assessment taken by all students. . . .

The Road Ahead

While 14 percent of U.S. elementary and secondary public school students are designated eligible for special education, these students are—first and foremost—general education students. . . .

As Congress works to update and refine NCLB, great care must be taken to maintain the accountability of special education students so that they may continue to experience rewards. Where roadblocks exist, equitable solutions can be forged. Separate systems serve no purpose, are open to abuse, and achieve less than acceptable results. Unifying and leveraging all available resources and raising expectations for all students can lead to significant improvement and close the achievement gap.

9

Special Education Students Do Not Thrive Under No Child Left Behind

Sherry Posnick-Goodwin for the California Teachers Association

The California Teachers Association, an affiliate of the National Education Association, represents more than 340,000 public school teachers, counselors, psychologists, librarians, other nonsupervisory certificated personnel, and education support professionals.

No Child Left Behind (NCLB) policies and sanctions are not helping students with special needs. For example, some teachers in Hesperia, California, have found that students with special needs are generally not identified as such because of NCLB guidelines and concern by school officials about how this labeling will impact schools' ratings under NCLB. Although they have implemented the ExCEL program, designed to provide individual attention for students in an effort to avoid the need for special education, many teachers have found it more problematic than the previous program because it wastes teacher skills and other resources. NCLB leaves special education students behind.

Scott Johnson's third-graders at Mesquite Trails in Hesperia [California] fold paper into geometric forms with ease—with the exception of a few students, including one little girl wearing a pink shirt and a puzzled look on her face.

"I don't get it," she says. She tries again and again, crumpling the papers into a pile as high as her frustration level.

Sherry Posnick-Goodwin for the California Teachers Association, "Are Special Needs Ignored in Effort To Raise Scores?" www.cta.org, 2007. Reproduced by permission.

Johnson believes she and a couple of other students in his class probably need special education services. But teachers like Johnson are being ignored when they voice their concerns.

"A lot of kids who need special attention don't get identified and don't get the help they need," says Johnson. "In many cases they're never referred to the Student Study Team (the first step in the identification process) when a teacher requests that they be tested. They are put in with all the other kids, and it's sink or swim."

Not Numerically Significant

Members of the Hesperia Teachers Association (HTA) believe the district is mixing special ed students with mainstream students so they will not constitute a "significant subgroup" and keep the whole school from making Adequate Yearly Progress (AYP) under No Child Left Behind.

"A year and a half ago, teachers were told directly in a staff meeting, 'Do not identify special education kids.' They said it right out loud in public," says HTA President James Pace. "This is coming from the district office. The reason given was that we do not want any significant subgroup in special education."

In California, a numerically significant subgroup constitutes at least 15 percent of a school's total pupil population and includes at least 50 pupils.

At Mesquite Trails, there are only 24 diagnosed special education students out of a total population of 727 students. And the district's other 10 elementary schools also have too few special education students to constitute a "significant subgroup." The closest would be Kingston Elementary, which has 49, just one short of significant.

Eight of the elementary schools made AYP [in 2006]. For those three that did not, special education students were not a factor.

Hesperia boasts higher API [academic performance index] scores and a 64 percent decrease in the number of students who are classified as "special education eligible," despite student population growth during the past decade.

Teachers believe the rising scores can often be attributed to special ed scores not being "disaggregated."

Concerned teachers believe their district has gone beyond the law's intent to the point where the students' needs are often not being met at all.

Grouping Children by Ability

Hesperia schools group children by ability as part of its ExCEL program, an "early intervention" program designed to meet every child at his or her individual level and avoid the need for special education.

"Many parents don't know what's going on," says Pace. "We have a high percentage of English learners. And no matter how you present it, no parent wants to have a child with disabilities." Parents are told their child is being grouped by ability instead of being labeled.

Each school has its own slightly different version of the ExCEL program, which groups students by grade level for language arts and math. Sometimes special education teachers teach these groups, which may include mainstream and special-needs children together. Other times, they're taught by mainstream teachers, even though the teachers may lack the proper training to work with special education students.

The law requires schools to provide special education students with the "least restrictive environment," but concerned teachers believe their district has gone beyond the law's intent to the point where the students' needs are often not being met at all.

"In many cases, students don't have the services they need to be successful in a regular classroom," says Pace.

ExCEL Has Flaws

At the district's middle schools and high schools, the ExCEL program means special-needs students may not get noticed for quite a while since teachers have up to 200 students in their charge, says Debby Shoemaker, a special education teacher at Hesperia Junior High.

[In 2006] her school placed all students in the Resource Specialist Program (RSP) in regular classes with no pullout program unless they were among the lowest students in a special day class. "Those with mild to moderate disabilities are often on their own."

After five years with the ExCEL program in effect in the district, secondary school teachers say they're not impressed with the results.

"These kids are failing like crazy," says Hesperia High School special education teacher Jim Garrett, referring to students who are moving up without having received special education services in elementary school.

Garrett, the union's grievance chair, believes the 20 percent dropout rate for the two comprehensive high schools can at least partially be attributed to the ExCEL program.

[In 2007] the Hesperia ExCEL staff will train about 70 school districts in the U.S. and Canada in how to use the program. [In 2006] the district helped implement the program in about 55 U.S. school districts.

Response to Intervention

This is part of a trend called Response to Intervention (RtI), which special education teachers fear may use special educators inappropriately, says Silvia L. DeRuvo, the immediate past president of the California Association of Resource Specialists and Special Education Teachers (CARS+). A member of the

California Faculty Association, she teaches future special education teachers at CSU-Sacramento.

The RtI model, which evolved from the reauthorization of the federal Individuals with Disabilities Education Act (IDEA), emphasizes early intervention and includes promising general practices for early intervention. But special educators are concerned that the bulk of the intervention responsibility will fall on their shoulders at the cost of time to support identified students.

[Teachers] fear that increasing pressure under NCLB will cause more school districts to use such programs [as Ex-CEL] to boost test scores.

Also, "when you don't identify many special education students, you can reduce your special education staff," says DeRuvo.

Because of the ExCEL program, Shoemaker believes she is underutilized as a special education teacher. "Honestly, I spend most of my day sitting in a regular classroom being used as an aide for any students who need help, not just special education students."

"The Ed Code specifies the specific caseload for resource teachers and is very clear about what that caseload is," says CTA Instruction and Professional Development Consultant Craig Nelson. "We're advising local associations to demand to bargain the impact of these changes."

Students' Needs Not Being Met

HTA President Jim Pace worries that some students aren't getting the services they need to succeed. While teachers are concerned about the impact of the ExCEL program on special education and mainstream teachers, they worry most about the impact on students whose needs are not being met. They fear that increasing pressure under NCLB will cause more school districts to use such programs to boost test scores.

When special education kids are being left behind, whether it's by not testing them or by not placing them in an environment where they can get the proper help they need, "it seems that NCLB isn't working," says Garrett.

"I just feel like a lot of these kids are being lost."

10

No Child Left Behind
Is Salvageable

Frederick M. Hess

Frederick M. Hess is a resident scholar and director of education policy studies at the American Enterprise Institute, a private, nonpartisan, not-for-profit institution dedicated to research and education on issues of government, politics, economics, and social welfare. He is coauthor with Chester E. Finn Jr. of No Remedy Left Behind: Lessons from a Half-Decade of NCLB.

As the No Child Left Behind Act (NCLB) nears reauthorization, it is time to focus on how the law can be reformed. Researchers reveal that there are eight major problems with NCLB that can be remedied. Part of the reason that NCLB has not been as successful as hoped for is that it is unrealistic; its requirements are not credible or easily enforceable; many states lack experts who truly understand NCLB's provisions; and there are no real consequences for failure. In addition, a lack of national standards, helpful interventions, adequate information exchange, and individual and school choice has led to a breakdown in the commitment that most districts have to the law.

Passed by Congress in late 2001 and signed by President George W. Bush one year after his inauguration, NCLB is the most ambitious federal education statute ever. It overhauled and expanded Washington's role in education; rewrote the rules; and set out to boost pupil achievement, narrow a host of "learning gaps," and assure every student a "highly

Frederick M. Hess, "Can This Law be Fixed?" *FrontPage Magazine*, September 4, 2007. Reproduced by permission of the author.

qualified teacher." Its hallmark is an historic attempt to impose a results-based accountability regime on schools nationwide. . . .

The political compromises that produced NCLB meant that its soaring aspirations were freighted with outdated machinery, weak sanctions, and uncertain interventions. Since unrealistic goals make failure inevitable, they have the perverse effect of focusing employees on complying and on keeping out of trouble. We sense—and fear—that NCLB's aspirational framework has created a system in which the prospect of likely failure by many schools gives educators more reason to focus on obeying rules and following procedures than on delivering results.

There is now enough mileage on NCLB's odometer to require a full inspection. Based on the research conducted for our book, *No Remedy Left Behind: Lessons from a Half-Decade of NCLB*, we found eight major defects in the current law's remedy scheme—and eight ways to fix it:

1. Get Real

With the gift of hindsight, educational accountability under NCLB turns out to be less about any conventional notion of school improvement or reinvention of government and more about fealty to a noble, even millennial aspiration. Rather than simply seeking to ensure that schools and districts effectively serve their students, NCLB's authors set the extraordinarily ambitious goal that every American child would be proficient in reading and math by 2014. In so doing, they took the language and mechanisms of standards-based education reform and married them to a policy agenda that owes more to Great Society dreams and the civil rights initiatives of the '60s than to any contemporary vision of disciplined education governance. In short, educational accountability à la

NCLB is more a form of moral advocacy than a sensibly designed set of institutional improvement mechanisms and incentives.

Federal policymakers ought to be more realistic about what they cause to happen in K–12 education, acknowledging that Uncle Sam is not adept at finely calibrated, escalating sanctions of the kind that NCLB expects states and districts to execute. Rather than imposing an incremental cascade of remedies, the feds should insist that states label schools that need help; act to strengthen those schools; and shut down, replace, or turn inside-out schools that resist improvement. That kind of mission is better attuned to Washington's strengths and more closely resembles the recipe that Uncle Sam has used to an excellent effect in reforming welfare. Simultaneously, choice programs should provide decent options to students—but for the sake of the children, not with an expectation that they will improve malfunctioning schools.

The goal is to empower hard-charging superintendents and principals—and to encourage others to charge harder.

---

2. Create a National Standard

Almost everywhere, compliance-style activity is underway as state and local officials attempt, sometimes cynically and sometimes in good faith, to fulfill NCLB's formal requirements and keep the money flowing. NCLB's remedies do not actually require states, districts, or schools to do better; they only require that states and districts comply with the statutory interventions. The law is frequently misunderstood as demanding student academic proficiency. In fact, it only requires compliance with the guidelines regarding reporting of data, spending, planning, and adoption of interventions. So long as officials do this, whatever their progress or non-progress in reading and math achievement, they are in compliance.

Washington should trust states to turn around their own schools, but all schools should be measured against a single set of national standards and uniform national tests, at least in the core subjects of math and reading. (This presupposes that such standards and tests can be competently and coherently designed—and not by politicians.) This would permit parents, educators, and officials to see clearly how their schools or states are doing. That strategy has the great merit of sorting out roles and responsibilities in the school reform domain, though we recognize that "national testing" will prove unpalatable to many Republicans and that "trusting states" will appall many Democrats. It is urgent, however, to distinguish the actions that the federal government can do well from those that must be entrusted to others.

3. Retain State Autonomy, but Implement Early, Authentic Intervention

NCLB's remedies are not, in fact, being used much (especially school choice and SES [Supplemental Educational Services]), or are being deployed in their mildest forms. Little NCLB-inspired choice is occurring, SES participation rates remain laughably low in most places, and there is scant evidence of systematic school restructuring. Nor do states and districts appear to have the capacity to restructure more than a handful of schools, and certainly not the hundreds—soon to be thousands—that the law has flagged as warranting such interventions.

Instead of mandating "one step per annum" over a seven-year sequence, NCLB should offer states and districts the option of interventions that span several years. For example, if a school fails to make AYP [Adequate Yearly Progress] (properly calculated) even for a single year, it would go into corrective action and its students would have access to SES and they would have the right to leave for other schools. This phase would last four or five years, during which time the state or district could do whatever it preferred to improve the school's effectiveness, and any federal rules, mandates, or spending restrictions that get in the way could be waived. The goal is to empower hard-charging superintendents and principals—and to encourage others to charge harder, knowing that Washington and their states would abet, rather than impede, them. For example, collective bargaining contracts that obstruct the reform of faltering schools should be set aside. . . .

By the same token, if the school does not begin to make AYP during that four- or five-year period of corrective action, the hammer would come down—no loopholes. After a certain point, when schools have gone several years without showing sufficient improvement, the interventions would be truly draconian. Such schools would be closed (with their buildings recycled to house new schools). In other words, a presumption of good intention in the initial years is appropriate, with the law providing essential political cover and local muscle to clear-eyed reformers. NCLB should therefore be designed to *replace* persistently ineffective schools.

4. Adopt Credible, Enforceable, and Fair Remedies

Education scholars David Plank and Christopher Dunbar suggest that the imagined threat of NCLB restructuring in Michigan has fostered a sense of urgency at low-performing schools. In some locales, it has brought an urgency and focus that had previously been lacking. It is possible that the actual design and operation of the remedies are not as important as their mere existence—and the mythology that envelops them. The problem is that this "Wizard of Oz" phenomenon—in which NCLB matters not for what it actually does, but because it creates a scary presence "behind the curtain" that can be used to prompt otherwise painful changes and be blamed for difficult decisions—may not last.

For any of this to work as intended, both parents and educators need to have confidence in the reliability of AYP as an identifying mechanism; any version of this scheme goes to pieces if states or districts are ordered to shutter schools that fair-minded observers regard as reasonably effective. AYP determinations must be better attuned to schools' effectiveness (i.e., "growth" or "value-added" as well as absolute performance) and better at distinguishing between schools in serious trouble and those that succeed with most of their students. (The administration's 2007 recommendations point toward the possibility of AYP "growth models" for all states; several states are piloting them today.) Right now, the law identifies hundreds of generally competent schools as failing, and pushes states either to set unrealistic targets that ensure that this designation will apply to many more schools or else to dumb down their standards. As long as NCLB ensnares relatively effective schools in a confusing web of remedies, it will prove difficult for even the best-intentioned implementers to make work.

NCLB's crude pass-fail grading system and its mandated restructuring are complicating homegrown improvement strategies.

In addition, the annual identification of school status needs to happen far faster than it does currently so educators, policymakers, and parents know a school's status well before the next school year begins. The incapacities of the testing industry must not be allowed to perpetuate the dysfunctional practice of delaying such information until August or October. *All* NCLB remedies require that a school's status be determined annually. Ensuring the accuracy of such determinations has combined with the failings of overburdened, underaccountable testing firms and balky data systems to produce an unworkable timetable. After the 2005–06 school year, sixteen states were unable to finish identifying their "needs improvement" schools before September—after the 2006–07 school year had already begun. For the interventions to work, states must radically alter their testing and data processes so that school identification is made—and publicly reported—in weeks instead of months.

5. Improve Information Flow and Compliance Monitoring

NCLB works very differently from state to state. In some states, its prescriptiveness impedes the state's own approach to standards-based reform, as in Florida, where NCLB mandates the restructuring of some schools that simultaneously earn honors grades from the state's accountability system. Certainly the federal law sows confusion where, as in California, there are discrepancies in school ratings between state and federal models. In particular, NCLB's crude pass-fail grading system and its mandated restructuring are complicating homegrown improvement strategies in such leading reform states as Florida and Massachusetts.

Parents, in particular, need better, faster, and clearer information about their SES and school-choice options. These remedies also demand the monitoring of SES providers, focusing on actual delivery of services, creating better templates for communication and evaluation, and supporting districts that do their best to make them work. States should conduct regular audits to encourage districts and schools to pay attention to customer service. It also makes sense to provide both SES and school choice simultaneously to students whose schools need improvement. A longstanding concern is the conflicted role that districts play as both SES providers and the "gatekeepers" charged with negotiating agreements with private providers. This arrangement asks districts to do unnatural things, work against their own interests, manage responsibilities for which they are not equipped, and engage in activities they regard as peripheral. The cleanest solution is for districts to stop controlling access to SES. Instead, states should explore how they could provide for other public or private entities to assume those responsibilities. Meanwhile, states must be required to monitor and report on the effectiveness of providers.

6. Promote More Choice More Often

Choice poses a particular challenge to school districts: they do not like losing money (which happens when parents send their children elsewhere or choose outside providers to deliver SES), yet they do not mind their teachers earning extra dollars on the side. Private tutoring providers are loath to be regulated by hostile state authorities and may not teach in ways aligned to district curricula or state tests, but they definitely want to maximize enrollment. Parents get their choice and SES information through the school, however, which has little reason to steer them to outsiders who would take district funds and not necessarily help schools make AYP. In the end, there has not been much competition, demonstrably effective remediation, or evidence of innovation.

If choice is to be a serious element of NCLB, as we believe it should be, the law's unworkable SES provisions need to be overhauled, and other choice options—including interdistrict choice, greater capacity via a flood of high-performing charter schools, and the inclusion of academically effective private schools—need to be seriously considered. The Department of Education must abide by its position that a lack of capacity is no excuse for failing to provide choices. Washington might require that districts find ways to offer more options—i.e., introducing virtual schooling, expanding the capacity of effective schools, or raising state charter-school caps—or lose federal dollars. It should, at the very least, make clear that states need to get out of the way and allow entrepreneurs to try to meet existing needs.

7. Provide Competent Help

Many states and districts need expert assistance to fix their troubled schools. Most lack such skill capacity. This is not just an education problem, of course. Yet we know of no sector, public or private, in which thousands of entities are each capable of assembling the know-how, talent, and organizational machinery to turn around troubled operations. Instead, such capabilities tend to be concentrated in a handful of organizations such as turnaround specialists and niche consultants.

If revitalizing low-performing schools is to occur with any consistency at scale, the nation will need to develop a set of effective operators capable of contracting with multiple districts or states to provide the oversight, leadership, knowledge, and personnel to drive restructuring. Operating on that scale will permit specialization and cooperation, and allow providers to build deep expertise. Washington cannot create this capacity, but it can provide resources, underwrite research, and encourage states to embrace nonprofit and for-profit entities that show a record of success.

8. Insist upon Real Consequences for Failure

The challenges posed by remedies raise fundamental issues of federalism as well as doubts as to whether the 1960s architecture, so reliant on state education agencies and local school districts for implementation, is even suitable for a reform regimen in which the behavior of those very agencies requires changing. Such steps require somebody to drop the hammer. Today, that somebody is the district, in the case of schools, and the state, in the case of districts. Yet neither hammer-wielder has shown much inclination to take politically tough action. Meanwhile, colleges of education have done an abysmal job of providing school or district leaders with the skills to turn around troubled schools, while licensure arrangements ensure that nearly all principals and superintendents are trained in those institutions. The threat of federal dollars being withheld is all but toothless, mainly because Congress restricted this penalty to "administrative dollars," and applied it only to failure to submit acceptable "plans" to Washington, not to weak academic performance.

In reauthorizing NCLB, Congress should introduce real consequences for failure and incentives for success. The law's current interventions create little urgency for individual educators or school or district leaders. Federal policymakers should encourage states and districts to adopt personal consequences for inadequate performance and failure to improve. Superintendents and principals should be held responsible for their schools' outcomes—rewarded when those outcomes are good, penalized when they are not. While many of today's calls for performance pay focus on rewarding teachers for test score results, the most fruitful place to begin is by ensuring that the executives have skin in the game.

11

No Child Left Behind Is Not Salvageable

Neal McCluskey and Andrew J. Coulson

Neal McCluskey is a policy analyst with the Cato Institute's Center for Educational Freedom for which Andrew J. Coulson serves as director. The Cato Institute is a nonprofit organization that focuses on public-policy issues and advocates for limited government involvement in the lives of Americans.

More than five years after the passage of the No Child Left Behind Act (NCLB), data reveal that at best the law has not helped the majority of American schoolchildren and at worst has hurt those students who are already at a disadvantage. While a number of persons and organizations have recommended changes to the law before it comes up for reauthorization in 2007, most of the proposed reforms merely replicate or extend the approaches set forth in NCLB, such as more testing and standards. Revising the law is not an option. In fact, the federal government should disengage from the education system and allow states to resume the role of managing the education of their residents.

NCLB's supporters began declaring the law a success within a few years of its January 2002 passage. . . .

Consider, however, that NCLB was passed in January 2002, and 4th-grade reading scores did not in fact change at all between 2002 and 2005. The one-point uptick between 2003 and 2005 only offset a one-point downtick between 2002 and

Neal McCluskey and Andrew J. Coulson, "End It, Don't Mend It: What to Do with No Child Left Behind," *Policy Analysis*, September 5, 2007. © Cato Institute 2007. Reproduced by permission.

2003. Furthermore, the Aspen commission [charged with evaluating the effectiveness of No Child Left Behind] neglects to mention that 8th-grade reading scores fell by two points after 2002. At least according to NAEP [National Assessment of Educational Progress] scores since NCLB's passage, it seems that the law has achieved nothing of consequence.

But postpassage scores don't tell us the whole story. To judge whether the law is working, we also have to look at pre-existing trends in achievement. It is quite possible, for example, that math scores were already rising, and reading scores stagnating or falling, before the law was passed and that NCLB affected neither. To have any hope of isolating NCLB's actual effect on student achievement and test score gaps, we have to compare score trends before and after the law's passage.

According to the NAEP Long-Term Trends report, 4th- and 8th-grade math scores did improve between 1999 and 2004, as did 4th-grade reading scores (8th-grade reading was flat). Attributing those results to NCLB is highly problematic, however, given that the law was only enacted in January 2002 and not fully implemented until the 2005–06 school year.

But suppose NCLB really did start transforming American education after just a year or two in existence. A rough idea of its effects could then be gleaned by looking at the standard NAEP mathematics and reading results (a data set that is separate from the Long-Term Trends report mentioned earlier). The news wouldn't be good. . . .

While both 4th- and 8th-grade math scores rose between 2003 and 2005 (the only period during which score changes can be reasonably attributed to NCLB), the rate of improvement actually slowed from that achieved between 2000 and 2003, a period before the law's effects would have been felt. In reading, the results were worse, with the period covered by NCLB seeing a score decline for 8th graders and stagnation for 4th graders, following an appreciable improvement between 2000 and 2002 (before the law's passage).

The analysis above is admittedly cursory, providing only tentative evidence of NCLB's effects. In June 2006 Harvard University's Civil Rights Project released a more rigorous review of NAEP score trends before and after passage of NCLB. After comparing the trends from 1990 all the way through 2005, the study's author, Jaekyung Lee, concluded that

- NCLB does not appear to have had a significant impact on improving reading or math achievement. Average achievement remains flat in reading and grows at the same pace in math as it did before NCLB was passed. In grade 4 math, there was a temporary improvement right after NCLB, but it was followed by a return to the prereform growth rate.

- NCLB does not seem to have helped the nation and states significantly narrow the achievement gap. The racial and socioeconomic achievement gap in NAEP reading and math persists after NCLB. Despite some improvement in reducing the gap in math right after NCLB, the progress was not sustained.

- NCLB's attempt to scale up the alleged success of states that already had test-driven accountability programs does not appear to have worked. It neither enhanced the earlier academic improvements seen in some of those states nor transferred them to other states.

NCLB supporters have responded to the Harvard study by ignoring it. At the time of this writing, the only reference to Lee's study on the Department of Education's website was its routine entry in the department's database of education research papers (the ERIC data-base). And although the Aspen commission lists the Harvard study in its bibliography, the commission's report does not address—indeed, does not even mention—Jaekyung Lee's findings. . . .

Evaluating Proposed Modifications to NCLB

In August 2006 Secretary [of Education Margaret] Spellings compared NCLB to Ivory soap: "It's 99.9 percent pure or something. . . . There's not much needed in the way of change." Given that there is still no conclusive evidence that NCLB is working, and that there is good reason to believe that it is producing harmful unintended consequences, this is not a common view. Even most NCLB supporters have called for the law to be reformed in various ways.

Recommendations for reform have generally taken a 'more of the same' approach.

Unfortunately, it is fair to say that, overall, recommendations for reform have generally taken a "more of the same" approach: more funding, more centralization, and more standards and testing. Consider, for example, several of the recommendations offered by the Aspen Institute in *Beyond NCLB: Fulfilling the Promise to Our Nation's Children*:

- Implement new requirements that principals qualify as highly effective principals (HEP), a designation that would carry licensure requirements, demonstration of "the necessary skills for effectively leading a school," and production of "improvements in student achievement that are comparable to high-achieving schools made up of student populations with similar challenges."

- Add science to the list of subjects on which students must make adequate yearly progress.

- Make public education address "students' behavioral and social needs by requiring schools to determine the availability of social services and mental health services when developing the school's improvement plan."

- Require states to add a 12th-grade assessment to their testing regime.

- Create federal "model content and performance standards and tests" in reading, math, and science and allow states to either adopt those standards and tests or have the federal government compare state standards and tests with the national model.

Evading Standards

To begin with, those requirements would add yet more stultifying rules and regulations to NCLB. That, however, is not their biggest fault. More important, none of those provisions would address a key problem with government-imposed education standards: evasion. The same authorities who have been keeping standards low and results "good" under NCLB would have power under the Aspen commission's proposals. There is no reason to think they would be any less likely to game the system under Aspen's proposals than under the current arrangement.

Consider nationalization of standards and tests. Intended to halt the race to the bottom by setting a single standard for every school in the country, federal standards would instead just relocate to Washington the political evasion game currently being played by states. Indeed, even if rigorous national education standards could initially survive the political process and be included in a revised NCLB, they would likely be crippled during the writing of regulations to implement the law, in which special interests have an even greater influence than they do in the legislative process. The work of writing regulations is done in the backrooms of the federal bureaucracy, not with the public scrutiny that often accompanies work on legislation, and interests like the National Education Association, which alone has a staff of more than 500 in Washington, are much better able to participate in such things as "negotiated rule making" than are parents.

Evasion would come from both the top and the bottom of the political food chain. At the top, an administration that championed the law would be encouraged by political expediency to produce favorable-looking test results to bolster its chances for reelection if in its first term, or to help its party—and the president's legacy—if in its second. Witness Secretary Spellings's pronouncements that NCLB is a proven success despite significant evidence to the contrary. At the bottom, interest groups like the National Education Association, National School Boards Association, and numerous others whose members might be embarrassed or harmed by higher standards would have a powerful incentive to lobby for lower ones. And regulatory bodies often come under the sway of the very groups they are supposed to regulate because those are the groups whose livings come from the status quo and are therefore the most active in lobbying, participating in such regulation-drafting activities as negotiated rule making and advocacy communications. As a result, the pressure on the bureaucracy to lower standards to present a favorable picture of student achievement would be just as intense at the national level as it has been at the state.

Involuntary National Standards

Unfortunately, the Aspen commission is not the only group on the national standards bandwagon. In January 2007 Sen. Chris Dodd (D-CT) introduced the Standards to Provide Educational Achievement for All Kids Act, cosponsored in the House by Rep. Vernon Ehlers (R-MI). The act would have the National Assessment Governing Board [NAGB]—which currently oversees the politically toothless NAEP tests—create national K–12 math and science standards and would bribe states to use those standards by establishing an American Standards Incentive Fund to pass out grants to states that adopted them.

State adoption of the standards is touted as "voluntary" by the act's supporters, but this claim rests on a fallacious equivocation: advocates seldom say *for whom* the standards would be voluntary. They would certainly not be voluntary for families. If a state opted in, as every state has opted in to NCLB thus far, families who did not agree with the law could not opt out. They would have no choice in the matter.

For states and school districts, too, national standards would not be truly voluntary. Dodd's incentive fund would, after all, be stocked with money taken *involuntarily* from taxpayers, and the federal government would return it only to states that "volunteered" to abide by the federal standards. That is more akin to extortion than voluntary exchange.

No matter how national standards were imposed, there would be nothing to prevent federal policymakers from playing politics with them.

Of course, real voluntarism would defeat the stated purpose of national standards, which advocates argue are needed to halt NCLB's race to the bottom. If states could truly opt in and out of such programs without penalty, then the sought-after uniformity in standards would not likely arise.

Playing Politics

The reality is that no matter how national standards were imposed, there would be nothing to prevent federal policymakers from playing politics with them, quietly dumbing them down just as states and local districts have done with their standards. Consider the national standards plan favored by the Thomas B. Fordham Foundation. It would vest standards-setting responsibility in an independent federal entity like NAGB, reasoning that doing so would greatly insulate the standards from political interference. NAGB, Fordham argues, "is a broadly representative and bipartisan body, with all key stakeholders present," and "it has not been timid about demonstrating its independence both of political masters and of education interest groups."

Of course, the NAEP—which NAGB oversees—has never had any real consequences (read: money) attached to its results, making it a very low-payoff target for special interests. In spite of that, Fordham president Chester Finn has himself told Congress that NAGB and other supposedly neutral federal education functions are in constant political peril. As he testified before the House Subcommittee on Early Childhood, Youth and Families in 2000:

> Unfortunately, the past decade has also shown how vulnerable these activities are to all manner of interference, manipulation, political agendas, incompetence and simple mischief. It turns out that they are nowhere near to being adequately immunized against Washington's three great plagues:
>
> - the pressing political agendas and evanescent policy passions of elected officials (in both executive and legislative branches) and their appointees and aides,
>
> - the depredations and incursions of self-serving interest groups and lobbyists (of which no field has more than education), and
>
> - plain old bureaucratic bungling and incompetence.

So even when no money has been attached to success on federal standards, according to Finn, NAGB has been under constant political assault.

Limit Federal Intervention

Another popular reform proposal is to add "flexibility" to NCLB—generally allowing schools and districts to more easily avoid the law's sanctions—while significantly increasing funding. A group of current and former school administrators called Public Schools for Tomorrow, for instance, recently called for much less standardized testing, as well as rewards for schools that make substantial progress (rather than sanctions for those that do poorly). They also, though, said that Washington should pony up money for a program to train new teachers and should fund NCLB at the full level authorized by the law. Congress, however, rarely appropriates the fully authorized amounts under any law.

Only two NCLB proposals break with the "more federal government" model. Instead of increasing the federal role in education, the Academic Partnerships Lead Us to Success Act of 2007 (A-PLUS) would allow states to declare that they want to run their own education systems and get money back from Washington if they do so. The Local Education Authority Returns Now Act (LEARN) would go one better, through a tax credit giving federal money directly back to individual taxpayers in states that declare their independence.

Neither federal interventions in general nor NCLB in particular have lived up to the expectations set out for them.

There are two versions of A-PLUS, with the Senate version requiring that states enter into performance agreements with Washington in exchange for their freedom and money. The House version requires no such agreement. The latter approach and LEARN are especially welcome because they would take federal politics out of setting performance standards. Only LEARN, though, makes whole the taxpayers from whom federal education money was taken in the first place. Still, all three are superior to other alternatives because they recognize that states are closer to their people, states are better equipped to handle education than the feds, and states that wish to run their own education systems should not have to sacrifice money taken from their taxpayers.

As preferable as those bills are to competing reauthorization proposals, neither is a complete solution to the federal education problem. While they decrease the compulsion and intrusiveness of current federal education policy, neither complies fully with the Constitution or eradicates the ability of federal policymakers to politicize educational decisions. . . .

Phase Out NCLB

Previous policy reports on the future of the No Child Left Behind Act have rested on the assumption that the law's basic principles are sound, and those reports have thus failed to critically examine NCLB's performance or long-term prospects for success. Worse yet, they have generally ignored important evidence that contradicts their assumptions.

The evidence and analysis presented here make it clear that the federal government has no proper role in American education beyond enforcing civil rights laws. Moreover, neither federal interventions in general nor NCLB in particular have lived up to the expectations set out for them. Nor can they, because federal intrusions actually discourage states from pursuing truly effective policies—those based on parental choice, school autonomy, and competition.

We therefore recommend that the U.S. Department of Education be abolished and that funding for all federal education programs be turned into temporary block grants to the states. Those grants should be phased out completely over three years, giving states time to reallocate their own personnel and resources. In addition, so that taxpayers do not continue to pay for a function Washington is no longer serving, federal income tax rates should be reduced in proportion to the amount of overall federal spending that is currently allotted to education.

One objection to this proposal might be that states have often proven little better at handling education than Washington. How will devolving power back to them help?

That is a reasonable objection. States have indeed been consolidating power over education at the same time as the federal government and have little more to show for it. And they have failed largely for the same reason as the federal government: while states are closer to the families who are being short-changed by public schooling, state governments are still huge political institutions dominated by special interests, and power is still held by politicians and bureaucrats, not parents. That is also true in many school districts, which have become much larger and more centralized over the last century. Some districts encompass entire counties, and large urban districts often have in excess of 100,000 students. New York City has more than a million. Even "locally," then, individual parents often have very little recourse when they are unhappy with the schools. That is why the public must demand that policymakers introduce universal choice at the state and local level once federal entanglement is removed.

Several states have already begun to move down the road to educational freedom through education tax credit programs (both for families' own use and for donations to scholarship funds that serve low-income families) and school voucher programs. Thus far, those programs are still too small to genuinely transform American education. The NCLB reauthorization debate, however, is an ideal time to pause, examine the evidence, and admit that school choice policies—not more centralization in Washington—are by far the most promising avenue for realizing our educational goals and ideals.

Organizations to Contact

The editors have compiled the following list of organizations concerned with the issues debated in this book. The descriptions are derived from materials provided by the organizations. All have publications or information available for interested readers. The list was compiled on the date of publication of the present volume; the information provided here may change. Be aware that many organizations take several weeks or longer to respond to inquiries, so allow as much time as possible.

American Association of Colleges for Teacher Education (AACTE)
1307 New York Ave. NW, Suite 300, Washington, DC 20005
(202) 293-2450 • fax: (202) 457-8095
Web site: www.aacte.org

The AACTE is the principal professional association for college and university leaders with responsibility for educator preparation. The AACTE maintains a national education policy clearinghouse and devotes several pages of its Web site to NCLB information and publications, especially in regard to the NCLB's impact on teacher education.

American Federation of Teachers (AFT)
555 New Jersey Ave. NW, Washington, DC 20001
(202) 879-4400
e-mail: info@letsgetitright.org
Web sites: www.aft.org; www.letsgetitright.org

AFT, an affiliated international union of the AFL-CIO, was founded in 1916 to represent the economic, social, and professional interests of classroom teachers and now also includes paraprofessionals and school-related personnel; local, state, and federal employees; higher education faculty and staff; and nurses and other health-care professionals. In addition to providing information and publications about NCLB on their main Web site, AFT also sponsors letsgetitright.org, a blog and Web site that focuses on reforming the NCLB. Some of the publications available through AFT include "NCLB: Its Promises, Its Problems" and "It's Time to Fix NCLB."

Commission on No Child Left Behind

One Dupont Circle NW, Suite 700
Washington, DC   20036
(202) 736-5800
e-mail: nclbfeedback@aspeninstitute.org
Web site: www.nclbcommission.org

The Aspen Institute's Commission on No Child Left Behind, a bipartisan, independent commission, was established to examine evidence about NCLB's effects and to make recommendations on how the law might be improved. On February 13, 2007, the commission released the results of all its data gathering: "Beyond NCLB: Fulfilling the Promise to Our Nation's Children." The report and many other documents are available on the commission's Web site.

Education Commission of the States (ECS)

700 Broadway #1200, Denver, CO   80203-3460
(303) 299-3600 • fax: (303) 296-8332
e-mail: ecs@ecs.org
Web site: http://nclb2.ecs.org

The ECS is an interstate compact created in 1965 to improve public education by facilitating the exchange of information, ideas, and experiences among state policy makers and education leaders. As a nonprofit, nonpartisan organization involving key leaders from all levels of the education system, ECS creates unique opportunities to build partnerships, share information, and promote the development of policy based on available research and strategies. The ECS maintains a database of NCLB resources, including information about Annual Yearly Progress reports, teacher quality, and testing.

International Reading Association (IRA)
800 Barksdale Rd., Newark, DE   19714-8139
(800) 336-7323 • fax: (302) 731-1057
e-mail: pubinfo@reading.org
Web site: www.reading.org

The IRA was founded in 1956 as a professional organization
for those involved in teaching reading to learners of all ages.
The IRA has devoted a large section of its Web site to NCLB
and the issues surrounding it. Some of its recent NCLB-related
publications include "Making a Difference Means Making It
Different: Honoring Children's Rights to Excellent Reading Instruction" and "No Child Left Behind: A Survey of Its Impact
on IRA Members."

National Association of State Boards of Education (NASBE)
277 S. Washington St., Suite 100, Alexandria, VA   22314
(703) 684-4000 • fax: (703) 836-2313
e-mail: boards@nasbe.org
Web site: www.nasbe.org

A nonprofit organization founded in 1958, NASBE works to
strengthen state leadership in educational policy making, promote excellence in the education of all students, advocate
equality of access to educational opportunity, and assure con-
tinued citizen support for public education. A large portion of
the NASBE Web site is devoted to NCLB. Some of its many
NCLB publications include "The No Child Left Behind Act:
What States Need to Know" and "Final Title I Regulations Is-
sued for No Child Left Behind Act."

National Center for Learning Disabilities (NCLD)
381 Park Ave. South, Suite 1401, New York, NY   10016
(212) 545-7510 • fax: (212) 545-9665
Web site: www.ncld.org

NCLD provides essential information to parents, professionals, and individuals with learning disabilities; promotes research and programs to foster effective learning; and advocates

for policies to protect and strengthen educational rights and opportunities. Since 1977, NCLD has been led by passionate and devoted parents committed to creating better outcomes for children, adolescents, and adults with learning disabilities. A large portion of NCLD's site is devoted to publications that investigate how NCLB serves children with learning disabilities, including "Why Students with Learning Disabilities Need No Child Left Behind" and "Making NCLB Work for Children Who Struggle to Learn: A Parent's Guide."

National Education Association (NEA)
1201 Sixteenth St. NW, Washington, DC   20036-3290
(202) 833-4000 • fax: (202) 822-7974
Web site: www.nea.org

The NEA is an international volunteer-based association of educators committed to advancing the cause of public education. A large part of its Web site is devoted to No Child Left Behind. Some of its recent NCLB publications include "NEA's Positive Agenda for the ESEA Reauthorization" and "Background on So-Called 'No Child Left Behind' Law."

No Child Left Inside Coalition
(410) 268-8816
e-mail: tackerman@cbf.org
Web site: www.cbf.org

The No Child Left Inside Coalition (affiliated with the Chesapeake Bay Foundation) is a national coalition of more than two dozen environmental and educational groups, representing hundreds of thousands of teachers, environmental educators, and others. The coalition was formed to alert Congress and the public to the need for public schools to devote more resources and attention to environmental education, especially through the reauthorization of the No Child Left Behind Act. The coalition's Web site offers talking points and other information about their environmental initiatives.

Rethinking Schools
1001 E. Keefe Ave., Milwaukee, WI 53212
(414) 964-9646 • fax: (414) 964-7220
e-mail: fred.mckissack@gmail.com
Web site: www.rethinkingschools.org

Rethinking Schools began as a local effort in Milwaukee, Wisconsin, to address problems such as basal readers, standardized testing, and textbook-dominated curricula. Since its founding in 1986, it has grown into a nationally prominent publisher of educational materials, with subscribers in all fifty states, all ten Canadian provinces, and many other countries. Rethinking Schools maintains an extensive collection of information regarding NCLB, including articles such as "Band-Aids or Bulldozers?" and "The No Child Left Behind Hoax," and the book, *Failing Our Kids*.

**Teachers of English to Speakers
of Other Languages (TESOL)**
700 S. Washington St., Suite 200, Alexandria, VA 22314
(703) 836-0774 • fax: (703) 836-7864
e-mail: info@tesol.org
Web site: www.tesol.org

Founded in 1966, TESOL is a global education association whose mission is to ensure excellence in English language teaching to speakers of other languages. It is especially interested in the NCLB provisions for English language learners (ELLs). TESOL maintains a clearinghouse of information and publications about NCLB and ELLs on its Web site, including "Position Statement on Teacher Credentialing for Teachers of English to Speakers of Other Languages in Primary and Secondary Schools" and "Position Statement on the Diversity of English Language Learners in the United States."

Bibliography

Books

Scott Franklin Abernathy — *No Child Left Behind and the Public Schools.* Ann Arbor: University of Michigan Press, 2007.

Lee W. Anderson — *Congress and the Classroom: From the Cold War to "No Child Left Behind."* University Park: Pennsylvania State University Press, 2007.

Ronald C. Brady — *Can Failing Schools Be Fixed?* Washington, DC: Thomas B. Fordham Foundation, 2003.

Frank Brown and Richard C. Hunter, eds. — *No Child Left Behind and Other Federal Programs for Urban School Districts.* Boston: Elsevier JAI, 2006.

Tim J. Carman — *Strength-Based Teaching: The Affective Teacher, No Child Left Behind.* Lanham, MD: Scarecrow Education, 2005.

Center on Education Policy — *From the Capital to the Classroom: State and Federal Efforts to Implement the No Child Left Behind Act.* Washington, DC: Center on Education Policy, 2003.

Nathan L. Essex — *What Every Teacher Should Know About No Child Left Behind.* Boston: Pearson, 2006.

Ken Goodman, ed. — *Saving Our Schools: The Case for Public Education: Saying No to "No Child Left Behind."* Berkeley, CA: RDR Books, 2004.

Laura S. Hamilton, ed. — *Standards-Based Accountability Under No Child Left Behind: Experiences of Teachers and Administrators in Three States.* Santa Monica, CA: Rand, 2007.

Frederick M. Hess and Chester E. Finn Jr., eds. — *No Remedy Left Behind: Lessons from a Half-Decade of NCLB.* Washington, DC: AEI Press, 2007.

E. Jane Irons and Sandra Harris — *The Challenges of No Child Left Behind: Understanding the Issues of Excellence, Accountability, and Choice.* Lanham, MD: Rowman & Littlefield Education, 2007.

Paul L. Kimmelman — *Implementing NCLB: Creating a Knowledge Framework to Support School Improvement.* Thousand Oaks, CA: Corwin, 2006.

Sunny Kristin — *Redesigning High Schools: The No Child Left Behind Act and High School Reform.* Denver: National Conference of State Legislatures, 2005.

Patrick J. McGuinn — *No Child Left Behind and the Transformation of Federal Education Policy, 1965–2005.* Lawrence: University Press of Kansas, 2006.

Deborah Meier and George Wood, eds.
Many Children Left Behind: How the No Child Left Behind Act Is Damaging Our Children and Our Schools. Boston: Beacon, 2004.

Derek Neal and Diane Whitmore Schanzenbach
Left Behind by Design: Proficiency Counts and Test-Based Accountability. Cambridge, MA: National Bureau of Economic Research, 2007.

Thomas S. Poetter, Joseph C. Wegwert, and Catherine Haerr, eds.
No Child Left Behind and the Illusion of Reform: Critical Essays by Educators. Lanham, MD: University Press of America, 2006.

W. James Popham
America's "Failing" Schools: How Parents and Teachers Can Cope with No Child Left Behind. New York: Routledge, 2005.

William J. Reese
*America's Public Schools: From the Common School to "No Child Left Behind".*Baltimore: Johns Hopkins University Press, 2005.

Alan R. Sadovnik, ed.
No Child Left Behind and the Reduction of the Achievement Gap: Sociological Perspectives on Federal Educational Policy. New York: Routledge, 2008.

Nancy W. Sindelar
Using Test Data for Student Achievement: Answers to "No Child Left Behind". Lanham, MD: Rowman & Littlefield Education, 2006.

Gail L. Sunderman, James S. Kim, and Gary Orfield   *NCLB Meets School Realities: Lessons from the Field*. Thousand Oaks, CA: Corwin, 2005.

U.S. Department of Education   *Building on Results: A Blueprint for Strengthening the No Child Left Behind Act*. Washington, DC: Education Publications Center, U.S. Department of Education, 2007.

Mary Konya Weishaar   *Case Studies in Special Education Law: No Child Left Behind Act and Individuals with Disabilities Education Improvement Act*. Upper Saddle River, NJ: Merrill/Prentice Hall, 2007.

Peter W.D. Wright, Pamela Darr Wright, and Suzanne Whitney Heath   *No Child Left Behind*. Hartfield, VA: Harbor House Law Press, 2005.

Mitchell L. Yell and Erik Drasgow   *No Child Left Behind: A Guide for Professionals*. Upper Saddle River, NJ: Pearson/Merrill/Prentice Hall, 2005.

Periodicals

Bill Archer   "But Who Fails with 'A' Grades? Public Schools Under Assault," *Daytona Beach (FL) News-Journal*, July 28, 2007.

Dan Berrett   "No One Answer to 'No Child Left Behind' Paradox," *Pocono Record* (Pennsylvania), April 9, 2006.

George Basler and Connie McKinney	"Are We Testing Kids Too Much?" *Binghamton (NY) Press & Sun-Bulletin*, September 2, 2007.
Joe Batory	"No Child Left Behind: A Misguided Federal Government Intrusion upon Public Schools," *Delaware County (PA) Daily Times*, June 10, 2006.
William J. Bennett and Rod Paige	"Why We Need a National School Test," *Washington Post*, September 21, 2006.
Jeb Bush and Michael R. Bloomberg	"How to Help Our Students: Building on the 'No Child' Law," *Washington Post*, August 13, 2006.
Kevin Carey	"No Complaint Left Behind," *Washington Monthly*, October 2007.
Anthony P. Carnevale	"No Child Gets Ahead," *Education Week*, September 26, 2007.
Esther J. Cepeda	"Now Needed: A 'No Teacher Left Behind' Law," Hispanic Link News Service, May 1, 2006. www.hispaniclink.org/newsservice/INDEX.HTM.
Zachary Coile	"No Child Left Behind Act Faces Overhaul, Political Donnybrook," *San Francisco Chronicle*, September 9, 2007.
Robert L. Cutts	"No Child Left Behind Good for Bureaucrats, Bad for Kids," *Nevada Appeal*, August 13, 2006.

D. J. Deeb

"No Child Left Behind Should Be Nullified," *Valley Patriot* (New England), April 2006.

Maureen Downey

"No Child Left Behind Needs Lift, Not a Recess," *Atlanta Journal Constitution*, September 17, 2007.

Ford Fessenden

"Schools Under Scrutiny over Cheating," *New York Times*, July 7, 2007.

Frank Fisher

"Should the District Dump No Child Left Behind?" *Park City (UT) Park Record*, September 28, 2007.

Bruce Fuller

"No Child Left Behind Lowers the Bar on School Reform," *San Francisco Chronicle*, June 16, 2007.

Amy Goldstein

"Mandate Aside, Private Tutors Aren't Always an Option," *Washington Post*, June 6, 2006.

Alis Headlam

"Put Education Back in the Schools," *Rutland (VT) Herald*, September 6, 2007.

Frederick M. Hess and Chester E. Finn Jr.

"Leave No (None, Zero, Nada) Child Behind?" Fordham Institute *Education Gadfly*, October 11, 2007.

Eugene Hickok and Matthew Ladner

"Reauthorization of No Child Left Behind: Federal Management or Citizen Ownership of K–12 Education?" Heritage Foundation, June 27, 2007. www.heritage.org/.

Danielle Holley-Walker	"The No Child Left Behind Act: Are We Saving or Ruining Our Public Schools?" Law.com, September 22, 2006. www.law.com.
Alison Lobron	"I'm Unqualified to Teach Your Kids," *Boston Globe*, May 7, 2006.
Jay Mathews and Karin Chenoweth	"Much Better than Adequate Progress," *Washington Post*, April 4, 2006.
Colman McCarthy	"Test-Driven Teaching Isn't Character-Driven," *Philadelphia Inquirer*, June 6, 2007.
Buck McKeon	"No Child Left Behind Reform That We Can All Support," *Hill*, September 18, 2007.
Bill Morem	"No Child Left Behind Isn't a Touchdown," *San Luis Obispo (CA) Tribune*, September 6, 2007.
Andrea Neal	"No Child Left Behind Sets Unreachable Goals," *Fort Wayne (IN) Journal Gazette*, July 13, 2006.
Lynn Olson	"As AYP Bar Rises, More Schools Fail," *Education Week*, September 20, 2006.
Margot Pepper	"No Corporation Left Behind: How a Century of Illegitimate Testing Has Been Used to Justify Internal Colonialism," *Monthly Review*, November 1, 2006.

Michael J. Petrilli   "What Works vs. Whatever Works: Inside the No Child Left Behind Law's Internal Contradictions," *Education Week*, July 26, 2006.

Mansel Phillips   "NCLB: The Worst in Rogue's Gallery of Bad Laws," *Amarillo (TX) Globe-News*, January 29, 2007.

Jason L. Riley   "A Law Best Left Behind," *Wall Street Journal*, September 28, 2007.

Carla Rivera   "Better Teachers, but Still Too Few," *Los Angeles Times*, April 12, 2006.

Scott E. Rixford   "Iraq vs. NCLB Benchmarks: Am I Missing Something?" *Education Week*, September 26, 2007.

Diana Jean Schemo   "It Takes More than Schools to Close Achievement Gap," *New York Times*, August 9, 2006.

Yvonne Siu-Runyan   "The No Child Left Behind Act—a Just So Story: The Lake Wobegon Effect," *Colorado Communicator* (published by the Colorado Council International Reading Association, Boulder, CO), July 1, 2007.

Gail Smith-Arrants   "No More Naps in Kindergarten," *Charlotte (NC) Observer*, May 1, 2006.

Joe Smydo   "No Child Left Behind Yields Progress, Setbacks," *Albuquerque (NM) Journal*, August 28, 2006.

Gary Stager	"My Plan to Fix NCLB," *District Administration Magazine*, August 1, 2007.
Julia Steiny	"Would Government Have Approved of Socrates, Merlin and Annie Sullivan?" *Providence (RI) Journal*, September 3, 2006.
Jennifer Toomer-Cook	"Advice to Congress: Dump Part or All of 'No Child Left Behind,'" *Salt Lake City Deseret Morning News*, June 1, 2006.
USA Today	"Two Views of NCLB," September 7, 2007.
Tim Walker and Alain Jehlen	"'Multiple Measures' Momentum," *NEA Today*, October 2007.
Peter Whoriskey	"Political Backlash Builds over High-Stakes Testing," *Washington Post*, October 23, 2006.
Ronald A. Wolk	"99.9 Percent Bunk: Why NCLB Is Far from Perfect," *Teacher Magazine*, October 1, 2006.
John Young	"Testing from Cradle to Grave," *Waco (TX) Tribune-Herald*, August 30, 2007.

Index